Modern African Writing

Comprehension and Appreciation

BRENDA COOPER

Longman

Longman Penguin Southern Africa (Pty) Ltd
Howard Drive, Pinelands

*Associated companies, branches and representatives
throughout the world*

First published 1984

ISBN 0 582 60995 X

Cover illustration by Petra Róhr-Rouendaal

Typesetting and reproduction by Pro-Set Flexoplate
Printed by Creda Press

Contents

Introduction

Modern African Writing is a selection of comprehension passages from a wide range of African writers. The importance of using African material in the classrooms and lecture theatres of Africa surely no longer needs to be pointed out. What does need to be stressed, is that the use of African material is not a magical key enabling African students to unlock their world and make sense of it. The continent is wide and varied, the writers differ on a number of issues and, moreover, the writing is quite difficult. Students will still have to work hard to 'comprehend'. A major goal of this book is to encourage them in developing a **critical** attitude to both the content and form of what they read. This, hopefully, will extend beyond this book. At the end of each chapter is a list of the books from which extracts have been taken. Students are strongly urged to read as many of these as possible.

Modern African Writing should be used flexibly, according to the needs of specific teachers and students. For example, themes can be selectively dealt with, passages within themes chosen and even questions within passages singled out. The book need not be seen as a whole course to be worked through religiously. Very broadly, the book is intended for the last two years of secondary school and the early years of University.

A wide range of ability is covered in the questions. However, some of the most difficult questions raised by the passages have been placed outside the main body of questions under **Further discussion.** These can be handled by teachers in many ways – class debates, splitting up into groups for discussion, written responses and so on. These passages are not intended to be tests completed by students entirely on their own. Some students might need more assistance than others. It is hoped that teachers will encourage classroom discussion, as well as provide guidance and support for students.

Wherever necessary students should be encouraged to use dictionaries. They must, of course, use their own words whenever they can as an indication that they understand what they have looked up in a dictionary or have read in a passage.

Some definitions, such as of *irony* or *symbolism*, are given in relation to the passages in which they occur. More background to these difficult concepts should be provided by teachers. Where important issues and/or literary techniques are dealt with only briefly in the book, they can be taken up and enlarged upon in discussion.

This is both a 'language' and a 'literature' book. A love of reading is possible only when one has the vocabulary to understand what is written and the critical ability to appreciate it. With these skills one can also enjoy writing on one's own – hence the **Creative writing** questions. The list of works from which the extracts have been taken is intended to encourage students to read further outside of this book. The writers are preoccupied with a desire to understand the history of their continent. So, surely, should African students be, in order to make sense of their writers. Some references to history books have been given to encourage background reading.

There is a possibility that the extracts can become divorced from the texts. To avoid this problem, passages have been chosen very carefully and every attempt has been made to remain true to the writers' attitudes.

Finally, please look at the following two pages for (a) some page references to terms and concepts like *metaphor* or *symbolism* and (b) a brief explanation of some of the terms used in order to ask the questions.

Terms and Concepts

A Some page references to terms and concepts

Tight definitions of terms and concepts have been avoided. This is because these are often complicated and used differently in different situations. What follows then are simply some references to concrete examples from the passages. It is hoped that by seeing these different examples a more complex understanding of these terms and concepts will emerge.

alliteration • question 8 after the poem *Stanley meets Mutesa*, page 22

caricature • Further discussion after passage *Portrait of a politician at home,* page 50
• question 5 after second extract from *Petals of Blood*, under *Names,* page 37

comparisons (metaphors and similes) • question 8 after passage *The Harvest,* page 8
• question 10 after passage *A South African Childhood*, page 16
• question 6 after passage *Stanley meets Mutesa*, page 21
• question 7 after passage *Education*, page 27
• question 2 after poem *Rulers*, page 46
• question 3a after passage *A Human Kingdom*, page 72
• question 2b after passage *Workers – 2*, page 94
• question 11 after passage *Marriage and Money*, page 100
• question 7 after poem *A Roadgang's Cry*, page 118

irony • question 3 after passage *Drought*, page 11
• question 10 after passage *Behind the Name*, page 40
• question 8 after passage *How to earn money*, page 55
• question 2 after passage *Nothing Changes*, page 67
• question 2 after passage *Boys or Girls?*, page 111

nostalgia • Further discussion after passage *The Rainy Season*, page 9
• Creative writing after passage *The Rainy Season*, page 9
• question 6 after passage *A South African Childhood*, page 15

paradox • question 10 after passage *The New Ilmorog*, page 61
• question 7 after passage *Marriage and Money*, page 99

pidgin • question 4 after passage *Food*, page 32

rhetorical question • question 8 after passage *Education*, page 27
• question 11 after poem *Song of Lawino*, under *Names*, page 35

satire • question 7 after passage *The Competition*, page 128

stereotype • question 2 after passage *Pianos and Drums*, page 26
• Further discussion after passage *Town life: Journalism in Johannesburg*, page 86

symbolism • question 1 after passage *Piano and Drums*, page 25
• question 9 after passage *Food*, page 32
• question 7a after passage *How to earn money*, page 54

B Some of the terms used in order to ask the questions

For a number of students this explanation will be unnecessary. It is given for those who will find it useful.

- Describe
- Give an account of . . .
- Find evidence for . . .
- How do we know that . . .
- Explain how . . .
- Rewrite in your own words.

Answers to these questions are clearly written into the passages and can be quite easily found on careful reading. In other words students must select the relevant part of the passage and show that they have understood it.

- What does the writer mean by . . .?

This type of question suggests that while the answer is to be found in the passage, there is some uncertainty as to the writer's meaning or at least some need to interpret it.

- Compare and contrast

Again the answer lies within the passage but the student has to organise the answer carefully. He/she has to select all those features that are common, and understand the important differences.

- Comment on
- Discuss
- Do you think the writer was correct in . . .?

Here the student has to build on and add to information found in the passages by including his/her own observations and thoughts.

- What do you imagine . . .?

While the passage provides the background to this type of question, the answer lies with the student. The student will have to be creative and draw on his/her own experiences.

- Is it effective?
- What is the effect of . . .?

These questions most often relate to figures of speech or the tools of language used by the writer. For example, there is comparison (metaphor and simile), symbolism, rhetorical questions etc. The student is being asked whether these tools have worked, have done their job properly. Their job is to make what the passage is saying better understood and appreciated by the reader.

2

Section A: History

Lonely Night   H. Budaza

The Past

The African past has been, and remains, a source of great inspiration to writers. It has been shown by some historians, however, that this can result in problems if it makes the writer unquestioningly assume (a) that the history of Africa stood still, and was the same throughout Africa for centuries before the Colonial period, and (b) that African society during this time was an earthly paradise in which there was complete harmony and equality among men and women. This section will look at ways in which a few writers describe the past in Africa. This theme, we will see, is bound up in some cases with that of childhood.

In the following passages you will find different opinions on the nature of African society as it was truly in the past, and as it is in much more recent times in areas relatively isolated from modern society.

You will have to decide which are the more realistic views. Try to read the works from which the extracts have been taken. (There is a list of books at the end of the section.) There is also a short list of history books that you might find interesting.

The Harvest

In our December, the whole world is in flower and the air is sweet: everything is young and fresh; the spring seems linked with the summer, and the country-side that for so long has been drenched in rain and shrouded in baleful mists now lies radiant; the sky has never seemed so blue, so brilliant; the birds are ecstatically singing; there is joy all round us – its gentle explosions are echoed in every heart. It was this season, this beautiful time of the year, that was stirring me so deeply, and the beat of the tom-tom and the festive air of our little procession moved me also. It was the best time of the year, the summer and all it stands for, all it holds and cannot hold – for how could it contain so much profusion? – and it made my heart leap with joy. . . .

My young uncle was wonderfully skilful at rice-cutting: in fact there was no one to touch him at it. I would follow proudly behind him, ready to take each sheaf as he cut it. When I had taken a sheaf from him; I would strip the stalks of their leaves then trim them all to an equal length and pile them up. And I would always take care to do this very gently, for rice is harvested only when it is very ripe, and if it is roughly handled the ears lose the best part of their grains. I did not tie the sheaves, for that was a man's job, but once they had been tied, I was allowed to go and put them on the great pile in the centre of the field. . . .

At midday, the women, bearing steaming platters of *couscous,* would leave the huts and walk in single file to the field. As soon as we caught sight of them, we would shout our greetings. Midday! It was midday! And work would stop all over the field.

'Come on,' my uncle would say.

And I would run along behind him.

'Not so fast!' I would say. 'I can't keep up with you.'

'Is there a hole in your stomach?' he would ask me.

'I could stable an ox in mine, I'm so hungry!'

And our appetites were in fact wonderfully whetted. However strong the sun, however furnace-hot the field with its dust and its quivering haze, it did not interfere with our appetites. We would squat down round the platters, and the hot *couscous,* made even hotter by the spices in it, would disappear, engulfed in great hungry mouthfuls, washed down by bumpers of cool water drawn from huge jars covered with banana leaves.

The break would last until two o'clock, and the men would spend the time sleeping in the shade of the trees or sharpening their sickles. Tireless, the young lads would play games or go and set snares; and though we would as usual make a lot of noise, we would take care not to whistle, because we were not supposed to whistle or pick up dead wood during the time of the harvest: such things would have brought misfortune to the fields.

The afternoon's work was much shorter and the time used to fly. It would be five o'clock before we knew it. The great field would now be shorn of its precious yield, and we would walk back in procession to the village – the tall silk-cotton trees and the wavering smoke from the huts seemed to welcome us from far off – preceded by the indefatigable tom-tom player, and singing at the tops of our voices the Song of the Rice.

Overhead, the swallows would already be skimming lower, though the air would still be clear as ever; but they, too, knew when the end of the day was near. We would go home contented, weary but happy. The good spirits had taken care of us: not one of us had been bitten by snakes that our trampling feet might have disturbed. The flowers, which would begin to unfold with the approach of evening, would be spreading their perfume on the air again, so that we walked as if attired in freshly-plucked garlands. If we had not been singing so loudly, we might have been able to hear the familiar sounds of the close of day: the shouts and laughter of women mingling with the lowing of cattle returning to their byres. But we were singing, always singing! Ah! How happy we were in those days!

CAMARA LAYE   *The African Child*

Questions

1 Explain in your own words how the rice is harvested.

2 Why did the writer think that the harvesting season was the best time of the year?

3 Find evidence in the passage that the narrator is describing his childhood.

4 How do we know that it is a childhood that has passed?

5 What did people feel would bring bad luck to the fields? Do you think they were right? Why?

6 a Name one hazard that the writer implies threatens people while walking out in the fields.

  b Can you imagine any other misfortunes that people might encounter during the harvesting season?

  c Why do you think the writer fails to mention any of these?

7 a Find **one** word in the passage that means each of the following:
  - soaked, made very wet
  - sunny and happy
  - prosperity – everything being plentiful
  - quickly swallowed up
  - tireless

  b What do these words share in common? Remember the writer's deep emotions in this passage.

  c Choose three of the words you have found and make sentences with them.

8 Writers often use comparisons so as to help us to picture more clearly what it is they are describing. For example, 'the country-side . . . shrouded in baleful mists' compares the depressing wintry mists to shrouds, or the sheets in which dead bodies are wrapped. Describe in your own words what is being compared in the following:
- stable an ox in mine (stomach)
- furnace hot
- shorn of its yield

9 a Can you think of simpler alternative words for the following?
   - platter
   - lads
   - attired
   - plucked
  b Do you think these are effective (useful) words for this writer to employ? Why?

The Rainy Season

Njahi was the season of the long rains. It was the favourite season with all the people. For then, everyone would be sure of a good harvest. The peas and beans, bursting into life, gave colour and youth to the land. On sunny days the green leaves and the virgin gaiety of the flowers made your heart swell with expectation. At such times women would be seen in their *shambas* cultivating; no, not cultivating, but talking in a secret language with the crops and the soil. Women sang gay songs. The children too. And the plants and all the trees around, swaying a little as if they were surrendering themselves to the touch of the wind, seemed to understand the joy of mothers. You could tell by the bright faces of the women that they were happy.

Not only the women but cows and goats caught the life. They jumped about, kicking in the air with their tails twisted into different shapes. The children were also happy and the ones who were grown up looked after the very young ones. You would see them running about, wandering aimlessly as if the madness or the intoxication of the bees had caught them. So they ran and played. But they were careful not to harm the flowers. Waiyaki could still remember how he used to follow his mother to the shamba and keep on climbing up a *mwariki* tree. Occasionally a delicate squeal of a neglected baby would be heard rising above the peace of the fields. And the voice of the mother, distant, yet ringing with life and deep concern, would rise, admonishing the bigger children to take care of the young.

In the evening all went home; husband and boys bringing in the cattle and goats; women bringing home the day's gathering of what would be eaten at night. They would then sit and wait to see what the woman of the house had for the evening meal. The boys usually talked. But the man of the house would sit under the family tree, if it was not yet dark, and meditate or hold a discussion with one or two elders who might call at that time.

JAMES NGUGI The River Between

Questions

1 How do we know that Waiyaki is reminiscing about his youth?
2 Ngugi is describing a great harmony between nature, animals and people. Find evidence for this in the passage.
3 a Ngugi indicates the existence of *a sexual division of labour* in the tribe. What work are the
   • women
   • men
   • children (and boys as distinct from girls) shown to do?
  b Ngugi hints at his own attitude to this division. Do you agree with him? Explain your own view.
4 What is a synonym (word with a similar meaning) for the following:
   • aimlessly
   • intoxication
   • concern
   • admonishing
   • meditate

Further discussion (See Introduction for use of this section)

1 Both passages can be said to be *nostalgic*. What is the meaning of that word?
2 In what ways are these passages nostalgic? How could
  a the nature of childhood and
  b the colonial invasion of Africa encourage a nostalgic portrayal of the past?
3 Ngugi has sometimes been criticised for describing the Kenyan countryside as if it were England rather than Africa. What do *you* think after reading the passage? Give examples from the passage to illustrate your opinion.

Creative writing

Think of a happy experience in your own childhood. Write a short description of it. Try to avoid the pitfalls (problems) of nostalgia.

Let us now look at some quite different perspectives on the past.

Drought

The land was ready and ploughed, waiting for the crops. At night, the earth was alive with insects singing and rustling about in search of food. But suddenly, by mid-November, the rain fled away; the rain-clouds fled away and left the sky bare. The sun danced dizzily in the sky, with a strange cruelty. Each day the land was covered in a haze of mist as the sun sucked up the last drop of moisture out of the earth. The family sat down in despair, waiting and waiting. Their hopes had run so high; the goats had started producing milk, which they had eagerly poured on their porridge, now they ate plain porridge with no milk. It was impossible to plant the corn, maize, pumpkin and water-melon seeds in the dry earth. They sat the whole day in the shadow of the huts and even stopped thinking, for the rain had fled away. Only the children, Neo and Boseyong, were quite happy in their little girl world. They carried on with their game of making house like their mother and chattered to each other in light, soft tones. They made children from sticks around which they tied rags, and scolded them severely in an exact imitation of their own mother. Their voices could be heard scolding the day long: 'You stupid thing, when I send you to draw water, why do you spill half of it out of the bucket!' 'You stupid thing! Can't you mind the porridge-pot without letting the porridge burn!' And then they would beat the rag-dolls on their bottoms with severe expressions.

The adults paid no attention to this; they did not even hear the funny chatter; they sat waiting for rain; their nerves were stretched to breaking-point willing the rain to fall out of the sky. Nothing was important, beyond that. All their animals had been sold during the bad years to purchase food, and of all their herd only two goats were left. It was the women of the family who finally broke down under the strain of waiting for rain . . . Each night they started a weird, high-pitched wailing that began on a low, mournful note and whipped up to a frenzy. Then they would stamp their feet and shout as though they had lost their heads. The men sat quiet and self-controlled; it was important for men to maintain their self-control at all times but their nerve was breaking too. They knew the women were haunted by the starvation of the coming year.

BESSIE HEAD   'Looking for a Rain God', from *The Collector of Treasures*

Questions

1 How do we know that there had been some rain a little while before?
2 The adults and the children are not shown to be in harmony with each other. Why is this so?

3 A writer is being *ironic* when she is saying more than is at first apparent, or is suggesting the opposite of what she seems to be writing. A writer does this in order to criticise something. In what way is Bessie Head being ironic when she describes the happy games of the girls as they look forward to making house and rearing children? (Think of what is happening in the rest of the passage as you answer.)

4 Before we hear that the women 'finally broke down' what evidence is there in the passage that the adults are going mad?

5 How do we know that the family are poverty-stricken and have no provisions saved up to see them through the drought?

6 a 'The sun danced dizziliy in the sky, with a strange cruelty. Each day the land was covered in a haze of mist as the sun sucked up the last drop of moisture out of the earth.' Comment on this description of the sun. What comparisons are being used? Are they effective? Why?

  b Now imagine that it has rained and write out two sentences of your own describing that rain.

7 What is the effectiveness of the repetition in 'waiting and waiting'?

Slavery

Amoo's daughter has been sold into slavery. He has been working with the wicked Momutu and his men in order to rescue his daughter.

By the time everything had been taken ashore it was quite dark. The prisoners were herded together and a guard set over them, although their hands and feet were still tied. Throughout the night their whisperings and sobs could be heard, punctuated now and then by the sharp crack of a whip. Some distance away, Momutu and his aides were reckoning up their haul, drinking quantities of spirits under the starry sky as they found how well they had done for themselves.

Momutu sent for Amoo to join them.

'You'll have a drink with us, won't you?' said Momutu when Amoo approached with his sleeping daughter on his back (but they only appeared as dim shadows).

'I must be going. I live a long way off and the coast isn't a safe place now. I've been working for you for two months,' said Amoo, refusing a drink.

'Is it true that you killed your wife rather than let her be taken prisoner by slave-traders?' asked one of the men, reeking of alcohol.

'Ahan!'

'And you've risked your life more than once to save your daughter?'

'She's my daughter! I've seen all my family sold into slavery one after another, and taken away into the unknown. I've grown up with fear,

11

fleeing with my tribe so as not to be made a slave. In my tribe there are no slaves, we're all equal.'

'That's because you don't live on the coast,' put in a man, which made Momutu roar with laughter. 'Go on, have a drink! You're a great fighter. I saw how you cut down that sailor. You're good with an axe.'

'Stay with me. You're tough and you know what you want,' said Momutu, passing the keg of spirits to him. Amoo politely declined a drink. 'This is our work,' Momutu went on. 'We scour the grasslands, take prisoners and sell them to the whites. Some captains know me, but I entice others to this bay and some of my men lure the crew off the ship. Then we loot the ship and get the prisoners back again. We kill any whites left on board. It's easy work, and we win all round. I've given you back your daughter. She's a fine piece and worth several iron bars.' . . .

Amoo could only see the whites of their eyes. He knew that these men would not think twice of seizing himself and his daughter and selling them to the first slave-trader encountered.

SEMBENE OUSMANE   Tribal Scars

Questions

1 Describe in your own words how Momutu and his men operate.

2 Why did a man like Amoo agree to work with Momutu?

3 How do we know that Amoo regarded death as preferable to slavery?

4 What is the effect on us of the sentence: 'Amoo could only see the whites of their eyes'?

5 Explain the metaphorical comparison in 'The prisoners were herded together . . .'. Is it an effective comparison?

6 The word 'entice' occurs in the passage. Find another word in the passage with a similar meaning.

7 a What are synonyms (words with a similar meaning) for:
   • haul
   • scour
   • loot?

   b 'Haul' is here used as a noun, and 'loot' as a verb. Can you make sentences with each of these two words using 'haul' as a verb and 'loot' as a noun?

8 Imagine that Amoo has returned to his tribe and is telling them about Momutu's invitation to join his band. That is, re-write the paragraph beginning 'Stay with me' in reported speech.

Further discussion

1 a Comment on and discuss Amoo's remark that 'In my tribe there are no slaves, we're all equal.'

   b What is the meaning of the slave-trader's reply that that was only because his tribe did not live on the coast?

2 It is not very common for an African writer to show how some Blacks (like Momutu) as much as some Whites were exploiters of the people. What is Sembene trying to stress here?

Creative writing

Write a short description of one of the following:
1 Amoo's killing of his wife to prevent her being sold into slavery.
2 Amoo's escape with his daughter from Momutu and his men.
3 Amoo's return to his tribe.

Age and Sex

The narrator is a town boy with a little bit of Western education, on a visit to the village of Kala:

When two men disputed the honour of entertaining me on any particular day, my uncle gave priority to the elder. This seemed only fair to me; I was still naïve enough to consider that the respect due to any person was in direct proportion to his age. Surely, I thought, that was obvious. Today I can see things more in perspective; and I can tell you without a shadow of doubt that my uncle wasn't nearly so disinterested in his motives as I was. Let me explain.

In general, a man's fortune – this word must be understood in its widest sense – was, in Kala, conditioned by his age. An old man was in a better position than a young one to give away a few head of cattle, thanks to a system which in the spheres of economics, law, and tradition alike was designed by old men, to benefit old men. As a result, an old man could always give more substantial presents than a young one. Besides this, there was the matrimonial system to be considered: this too was biased in favour of age, so that a young man had less chance of getting *married* than his elders. As a result, in Kala a woman is an infallible sign of male prosperity, equivalent to a good refrigerator and automobile in America. And, just as in America, it's not enough for a Babbitt to be a successful businessman or have a substantial sum in the bank. He must prove the fact by showing off his fridge and his Chrysler; if he doesn't, people look down on him. In the same way, it was essential to be married in Kala if you wanted public esteem.

My uncle, who was not only a social conformer of the most abject kind, but also tended to look well ahead, thus always gave preference to older claimants. There were an extraordinary number of old people living in Kala.

To look at the problem from a different angle for a moment, Kala was, as I think I have already said, a really enormous village. It was quite clear to me that if I stayed on for a whole year the old folk would still be monopolizing me, while their juniors would be getting resentful and frustrated. That, in fact, was exactly what happened.

MONGO BETI *Mission to Kala*

Questions

1 Why do you think there is such competition to entertain the narrator?

2 What do you think his uncle hoped to gain in all this?

3 Write out the sentence that shows that the narrator used to believe that older people deserved more privileges than younger ones. What do *you* think? Why?

4 Why was the quality of life of an old man in Kala better than that of a young one?

5 Re-write in your own words the phrase '. . . a system which in the spheres of economics, law, and tradition alike was designed by old men, to benefit old men.'

6 Why did a young man have less chance of getting married than an old one?

7 What, according to the narrator, was the position of women in Kala?

8 In what way did the narrator's visit begin to cause discord (trouble) in the village?

9 What is a 'social conformer of the most abject kind'?

Further discussion

Remember Amoo's comment in the last passage that there was equality in his tribe because there were no slaves. Do you think there can be said to be inequality in a village if there are these age and sex distinctions described by Beti? Why?

A South African Childhood

I have never known why we – my brother, sister and I – were taken to the country when I was five. We went to live with our grandmother – paternal grandmother. My father and mother remained in Pretoria where they both worked, my father a shop messenger in an outfitters' firm; Mother as a domestic servant. That was in the autumn of 1924.

I remember feeling quite lost during the first weeks in that little village of Maupaneng, seventy-five miles out of Pietersburg town; a village of about 5 000 people. My grandmother sat there under a small lemon tree next to the hut, as big as fate, as forbidding as a mountain, stern as a mimosa tree.

She was not the smiling type. When she tried, she succeeded in leering muddily. But then she was not the crying type either: she gave her orders sharp and clear. Like the sound she made when she pounded on the millstone with a lump of iron to make it rough enough for grinding on. I do not remember ever being called gently by her. One of her two daughters was the spit of her; the other anaemic and fawning. But they seldom came home. They worked in Pretoria. When they were not working they had children without being able to secure a man they could really call a husband. I haven't seen them or my grandmother now for the last twenty years, although I know they are still alive.

Things stand out clearly in my mind from those years: my granny, the mountain on the foot of which the village clung like a leech, and the mountain darkness, so solid and dense. And my granny seemed to conspire with the mountain and the dark to frighten us . . .

Looking back to those first thirteen years of my life – as much of it as I can remember – I cannot help thinking that it was time wasted. I had nobody to shape them into a definite pattern. Searching through the confused threads of that pattern a few things keep imposing themselves on my whole judgement. My grandmother; the mountain; the tropical darkness which glow-worms seemed to try in vain to scatter; long black tropical snakes; the brutal Leshoana river carrying on its broad back trees, cattle, boulders; world of torrential rains; the solid shimmering heat beating down on yearning earth; the romantic picture of a woman with a child on her back and an earthen pot on her head, silhouetted against the mirage.

But all in all perhaps I led a life shared by all other country boys. Boys who are aware of only one purpose of living; to be.

EZEKIEL MPHAHLELE *Down Second Avenue*

Questions

1 Why did the writer's parents and aunts all live in Pretoria?
2 Describe the reasons why the writer was unhappy in the village of Maupaneng.
3 Find evidence for the fact that the writer is portraying a breakdown in family life. (Think of both his own situation and that of his aunts.)
4 Re-write in your own words the sentence: 'And my granny seemed to conspire with the mountain and the dark to frighten us.'
5 Describe in your own words the type of woman his grandmother was.
6 Study the description of the woman with a child on her back. How do we know that Mphahlele is aware of the problems of nostalgia that we discussed earlier?
7 What is a 'paternal' as opposed to a 'maternal' grandmother?
8 What is 'the spit of her' short for? What does the phrase mean?

9 Explain the meaning of the sentence 'Boys who are aware of only one purpose of living; to be.'

10 This writer uses a lot of similes in this passage. These are comparisons which are made obvious by the use of 'like' or 'as'. Can you explain what characteristics are being compared in the following similes:
  - as big as fate
  - as forbidding as a mountain
  - stern as a mimosa tree
  - . . . the mountain on the foot of which the village clung like a leech . . .

11 What do we call a work, like *Down Second Avenue,* in which a writer tells us his own life-story?

Further discussion

Mphahlele's childhood memories are much less happy than those of some of the other writers we have looked at. Do you think this can be related to the fact that he grew up in South Africa? Why?

Book list

CAMARA LAYE *The African Child,* Fontana, 1959, pp. 46-8 & 53-4.

JAMES NGUGI *The River Between,* Heinemann, 1965, pp. 91-2.

BESSIE HEAD 'Looking for a Rain God' in *The Collector of Treasures,* Heinemann, 1977, pp. 58-9.

SEMBENE OUSMANE 'Tribal Scars' in *Tribal Scars,* Heinemann, 1962, pp. 106-8.

MONGO BETI *Mission to Kala,* Heinemann, 1964, pp. 99-100.

EZEKIEL MPHAHLELE *Down Second Avenue,* Faber & Faber, 1959, pp. 11 & 18-19.

Useful History books

BASIL DAVIDSON *Africa in Modern History,* Pelican Books, 1978.

ROBIN HALLET *Africa to 1875,* University of Michigan Press, 1970.

ROBIN HALLET *Africa Since 1875,* University of Michigan Press, 1974.

A.G. HOPKINS *An Economic History of West Africa,* Longman, 1973.

R. OLIVER & J.D. FAGE *A Short History of Africa,* Penguin, 1962.

Long Journey   H. Budaza

Change

The causes and results of the penetration by European powers of the African continent are complicated.

Colonialism, as this penetration became known, took different forms, depending upon which European power and which African territory were concerned. But the similarities in causes and results of colonialism were probably even greater. Africa was now drawn much more sharply into the world economic system. And it has been shown that, because of its more advanced stage of industrialisation, and more developed technology, Europe was able to decide the terms of Africa's entry into the international economy. A small section of the African people was needed to assist the colonisers. This small section benefitted. However, the majority of African people suffered under this system of colonialism or imperialism. Imperialism is the term used when there is some understanding of the ways in which the colonising powers gained from the taking of colonies. Most African writers have been concerned with the subject of colonialism, and many have written about it. Their main interest, however, has seemed to lie with changes that were brought about in customs – lifestyles, dress, values, food etc. Only a few writers have been concerned with the deeper economic and social changes that came with colonialism.

*There obviously **were** these cultural changes and writers are often the best people to record them. The danger that some historians have pointed to is that readers can be led to believe that colonialism was **caused** by the West's desire to 'civilise' Africans – that is, by the desire to change their religion, food, dress and customs, rather than by the coming of a certain stage in Europe's economic development which made colonies desirable. What do **you** think?*

Stanley meets Mutesa

Such a time of it they had;
The heat of the day
The chill of the night
And the mosquitoes that followed.
Such was the time and
They bound for a kingdom.

The thin weary line of carriers
With tattered dirty rags to cover their backs;
The battered bulky chests
That kept on falling off their shaven heads.
Their tempers high and hot
The sun fierce and scorching
With it rose their spirits
With its fall their hopes
As each day sweated their bodies dry and
Flies clung in clumps on their sweat-scented backs.
Such was the march
And the hot season just breaking.

Each day a weary pony dropped,
Left for the vultures on the plains;
Each afternoon a human skeleton collapsed,
Left for the Masai on the plains;
But the march trudged on
Its Khaki leader in front
He the spirit that inspired.
He the light of hope.

Then came the afternoon of a hungry march,
A hot and hungry march it was;
The Nile and the Nyanza
Lay like two twins
Azure across the green countryside.
The march leapt on chaunting
Like young gazelles to a water hole.
Hearts beat faster
Loads felt lighter
As the cool water lapt their sore soft feet.
No more the dread of hungry hyenas
But only tales of valour when
At Mutesa's court fires are lit.
No more the burning heat of the day
But song, laughter and dance.

The village looks on behind banana groves,
Children peer behind reed fences.
Such was the welcome
No singing women to chaunt a welcome
Or drums to greet the white ambassador;
Only a few silent nods from aged faces
And one rumbling drum roll
To summon Mutesa's court to parley
For the country was not sure.

The gate of reeds is flung open,
There is silence
But only a moment's silence –
A silence of assessment.
The tall black king steps forward,
He towers over the thin bearded white man
Then grabbing his lean white hand
Manages to whisper
'Mtu Mweupe Karibu'
White man you are welcome.
The gate of polished reed closes behind them
And the west is let in.

DAVID RUBADIRI   Stanley meets Mutesa in *A book of African Verse*

Questions

1 Describe in your own words the difficulties encountered and hardships endured by the marchers to Mutesa's court.
2 Why are the people who collapsed on the way referred to as 'skeletons'?
3 How do we know that Stanley was a good leader on the march?
4 a How do we know that the welcome given by the village to Stanley and his party was somewhat half-hearted?
  b Write out the words that show that even Mutesa was uncertain as to whether to welcome them.
  c Do you think the people were correct to be suspicious? Why?
5 a What is the meaning of *ambassador?*
  b Write out a line that tells us for whom Stanley was an ambassador.
6 There is not much reliance on figurative language (metaphors and similes) in this poem. There are, however, one or two similes. Can you find one of these, explain in your own words what is being compared and say whether the comparison is effective?
7 What Rubadiri does use quite frequently is two short lines that are paired for contrast or correspondence – e.g.
'The heat of the day
The chill of the night.'

a Can you find two other examples of this?
b Try and think of a reason why a poet uses this device and whether it is effective.
8 Another device used by this poet is that of *alliteration* – i.e. the use of words that begin with the same letter. For example:
The <u>b</u>attered <u>b</u>ulky chests.
Can you find two other examples of this?
9 Why do you think poets use language devices like these we have seen in this poem? In other words, do they add to their poetry?

The Portuguese in Angola

The following incident describes the arrest of Domingos:

And it was already nine o'clock at night, with the full moon over the *sanzala* silvering the fast waters of the Kuanza between the hills, when the sound of a truck by the huts put fear into the hearts of mothers and sweethearts. The blue truck was the enemy; whenever it came, someone would go bound and battered on the back of the truck to the town. Then, bang! He did not return or he returned all beaten up with hands and feet swollen. Once the truck began a round of the encampment, like a kite hovering over young chickens, no father knew any more if on the next day he would see his son return from work; or clock in; or answer the foreman's morning roll-call.

Small lamps were lit, mothers with their babies peered fearfully from doorways. The truck had already stopped, with its headlights pointed at Domingos' hut, and the *cipaios**** were banging their truncheons on the door and bellowing for it to be opened. The Cadet, who had come at the wheel, stood a little way back, holding a pistol.

And that night the people saw Domingos come out, still buttoning his trousers, with his eyes almost blinded by the truck's headlights; the beating began inside the hut, with Maria in tears and the child Sebastian awoken and wailing. Two *cipaios* held the tractor driver while a third covered him with punches and kicks. Domingos Xavier, a tall, thin man, bowed deeply in instinctive self-defence, and still tried to run back to his *companheira*, but the Cadet gave him a quick tap on the neck with the pistol butt. The *cipaios,* grabbing him by arms and legs, threw him onto the back of the truck . . .

---

* *cipaio* – an African recruited to serve in a subordinate role with the Portuguese colonial police.

The tortured body of the tractor driver had fallen on top of prisoners who were already sleeping at that hour of the night. Just before dawn, when the silence covered all other sounds, the clanging of the great door woke the prisoners, who remained with eyes open, trying to make out in the dark who had been brought there. They heard the *cipaio* turning the main lock, shooting the bar, and then leaving while talking quietly with someone else.

A strong moon shone in a cloudless but starry sky and the white light flooded through a window to wash over the bodies stretched out on the ground. There were many, without a bed, sleeping in heaps on the bare cement, or wrapped in rags and old blankets. Servants brought by their bosses, unemployed men caught without a signature on their work pass, drunks taken up at the ever-open doors of the taverns, petty thieves, rowdies, united in a common fate of a beating and forced work on the roads. The arrival of another prisoner was always treated casually, someone might mutter something, but no one wanted to show concern to the *cipaios*. Only in the morning before they went off to forced labour would they see who the unlucky man was.

But as soon as the *cipaios'* footsteps could no longer be heard and the silence had returned, the prisoners woken by the falling of a body on top of them got up in surprise that this countryman did not even stir . . .

From all corners of the prison people came to sit in silence round the dying brother. One lad took off his old jacket and used it to cover the tractor driver's bruised and broken chest. Only the face was now uncovered, bathed in the moonlight coming through the window. The old man went on whimpering in the corner. The moon peered through the crevices and the high windows apologetically to cover the serence and tranquil face of Domingos Xavier.

JOSÉ LUANDINO VIEIRA   *The Real Life of Domingos Xavier*

Questions

1 Why was the blue truck the enemy?

2 How do we know that there were mainly workers and their families living in the encampment?

3 Can you imagine why the Portuguese sent *cipaios* to pick up prisoners in the way described, rather than coming themselves?

4 Why do you think men agreed to become *cipaios*?

5 Domingos Xavier was arrested for political reasons. What do you think that meant during the period of Portuguese occupation of Angola?

6 Give two examples from the passage which show that the people tried to give each other support and assistance.

7 a What do you think the authorities were trying to obtain from Domingos Xavier by treating him so brutally?

   b Why do you think his face is described as 'serene and tranquil'?

23

8 a For what offences are other prisoners in jail?
  b What do you think the writer feels about these offences?
  c In what way does it benefit the colonial authorities to round up these
     prisoners?
9 Explain the comparison made in the following simile: '. . . the truck
   began a round of the encampment, like a kite hovering over young
   chickens, . . .' Is it effective? Why?
10 Make sentences with the following words:
   • peered
   • bellowing
   • mutter
   • whimpering
   • crevices

Further discussion

1 Vieira, among other African writers, portrays colonialism as the
   ruthless and cruel exploitation of African people. What do *you* think?
2 Vieira shows that some blacks joined up with the White colonialists
   (remember the *cipaios*), and Vieira is himself a White man who fought
   against colonialism. What do you think is the significance of this?

Creative writing

1 Domingos Xavier's wife, Maria, travels to Luanda with her baby in
   order to try and find out from the authorities where her husband is being
   kept and to attempt to see him. Give a short imaginary description of her
   experiences. (You are not expected to have any knowledge of Angola in
   your answer.)

   or

2 Write a poem portraying the advent (arrival) of colonialism in Africa. In
   your poem you could give a general picture of colonialism, or you could
   concentrate on one aspect of colonialism.

*Many African writers describe the advent of colonialism mainly in terms of
the clashing of two cultures, Western and African. They are especially
critical of Africans who try to imitate or 'ape' Western customs and ways.
Let us look at some examples of this.*

Piano and Drums

When at break of day at a riverside
I hear jungle drums telegraphing
the mystic rhythm, urgent, raw
like bleeding flesh, speaking of
primal youth and the beginning,
I see the panther ready to pounce,
the leopard snarling about to leap
and the hunters crouch with spears poised;

And my blood ripples, turns torrent,
topples the years and at once I'm
in my mother's lap a suckling;
at once I'm walking simple
paths with no innovations,
rugged, fashioned with the naked
warmth of hurrying feet and groping hearts
in green leaves and wild flowers pulsing.

Then I hear a wailing piano
solo speaking of complex ways
in tear-furrowed concerto;
of far-away lands
and new horizons with
coaxing diminuendo, counterpoint,
crescendo. But lost in the labyrinth
of its complexities, it ends in the middle
of a phrase at a daggerpoint.

And I lost in the morning mist
of an age at a riverside keep
wandering in the mystic rhythm
of jungle drums and the concerto.

GABRIEL OKARA   Piano and Drums in *Modern Poetry from Africa*

Questions

1 A *symbol* stands for, or represents something else. Its aim is to help us
to understand the other thing better. The symbol is similar in some or
other way to what it represents. It becomes a striking image which
readily comes to our minds. In this poem, for example, the poet has used
drums as the symbol of African culture and the piano as the symbol of
Western culture. Describe in your own words the nature of these two
cultures as portrayed by the poet through these symbols.

2 A danger in the use of symbolism is that it can over-simplify and even distort what it is symbolising. Symbolism can lead to stereotyping. Think of the meaning of a *stereotype* – a much repeated, unquestioned view of something that no longer tells us anything very meaningful about it.
Do you think that Okara's symbols stereotype African and Western culture? What, for example, do you think of the 'simple paths with no innovations' of African culture, and the 'labyrinth of complexities' of Western? Take other examples from the poem for your answer.

3 What are the meanings of the following? You can use your dictionary to help you, but look especially at how these words are used in the poem to give you clues as to their meaning:
  • the mystic rhythm
  • primal youth
  • rugged
  • diminuendo, counterpoint, crescendo

4 Explain the comparisons in the following. Say whether they are metaphors or similes and if you think they are effective and why:
  • drums . . . raw/like bleeding flesh
  • my blood ripples, turns torrent
  • wild flowers pulsing
  • wailing piano
  • tear-furrowed concerto

5 Why does the writer describe himself as lost?

Education

The following extract describes education in a French African colony:

Fathers used to take their children to school as they might lead sheep into a slaughterhouse. Tiny tots would turn up from backwood villages thirty or forty miles up-country, shepherded by their parents, to be put on the books of some school, it didn't matter which. They formed a miserable floating population, these kids: lodged with distant relations who happened to live near the school, underfed, scrawny, bullied all day by ignorant monitors. The books in front of them presented a universe which had nothing in common with the one they knew: they battled endlessly with the unknown, astonished and desperate and terrified.

We were those children – it is not easy to forget – and it was our parents who forced this torment upon us. Why did they do it?

We were catechized, confirmed, herded to Communion like a gaggle of holy-minded ducklings, made to confess at Easter and on Trinity Sunday, to march in procession with banners on the Fourteenth of July; we were militarized, shown off proudly to every national and international commission.

That was us. Remember?

Ragged, rowdy, boastful, nit-infested, cowardly, scab-ridden, scrounging little beasts, feet swollen with jiggers: that was us, a tiny squeaking species adrift in the modern age like poultry in mid-Atlantic. What god were we being sacrificed to, I wonder?

MONGO BETI   Mission to Kala

Questions

1 Why did it not matter which school the children were enrolled at?
2 Why are they described as a floating population?
3 Write out a sentence that tells us that the children did not learn much that was useful to their lives, at school.
4 How do we know that the writer did not think that the children were given meaningful religious guidance either?
5 Why do you think that the children were 'shown off'?
6 Find evidence in the passage that the writer also blamed parents for their children's suffering.
7 The writer makes much use of simile.
  a What do the following similes have in common?
  b Explain the meaning of each one separately:
    • 'Fathers used to take their children to school as they might lead sheep into a slaughterhouse'
    • 'We were catechized, confirmed, herded to Communion like a gaggle of holy-minded ducklings, . . .'
    • '. . . a tiny squeaking species adrift in the modern age like poultry in mid-Atlantic.'
8 *A rhetorical question* is one to which an immediate reply is not expected.
  a Find three examples of rhetorical questions in this passage.
  b What effect does this device have?

Further discussion

What do you think these children might have enjoyed learning about at school? Why?

Courtship

Lakunle, the partially educated village school teacher is courting Sidi, the village beauty:

SIDI   You talk and talk and deafen me
With words which always sound the same
And make no meaning.
I've told you, and I say it again
I shall marry you today, next week
Or any day you name.
But my bride-price must first be paid.
Aha, now you turn away.
But I tell you, Lakunle, I must have
The full bride-price. Will you make me
A laughing-stock? Well, do as you please.
But Sidi will not make herself
A cheap bowl for the village spit.

LAKUNLE   On my head let fall their scorn.

SIDI   They will say I was no virgin
That I was forced to sell my shame
And marry you without a price.

LAKUNLE   A savage custom, barbaric, out-dated,
Rejected, denounced, accursed,
Excommunicated, archaic, degrading,
Humiliating, unspeakable, redundant.
Regressive, remarkable, unpalatable.

SIDI   Is the bag empty? Why did you stop?

LAKUNLE   I own only the Shorter Companion
Dictionary, but I have ordered
The Longer One – you wait!

SIDI   Just pay the price.

LAKUNLE   (with a sudden shout.)
An ignoble custom, infamous, ignominious
Shaming our heritage before the world.
Sidi, I do not seek a wife
To fetch and carry,
To cook and scrub,
To bring forth children by the gross . . .

SIDI   Heaven forgive you! Do you now scorn
Child-bearing in a wife?

LAKUNLE   Of course I do not. I only mean . . .
Oh Sidi, I want to wed
Because I love,
I seek a life-companion . . .
(Pulpit declamatory.)
'And the man shall take the woman
And the two shall be together
As one flesh'.'

28

	Sidi, I seek a friend in need.
	An equal partner in my race of life.
SIDI	Then pay the price.
LAKUNLE	Ignorant girl, can you not understand?
	To pay the price would be
	To buy a heifer off the market stall.
	You'd be my chattel, my mere property.
	No, Sidi!
	When we are wed, you shall not walk or sit
	Tethered, as it were, to my dirtied heels.
	Together we shall sit at table
	– Not on the floor – and eat,
	Not with fingers, but with knives
	And forks, and breakable plates
	Like civilized beings.
	I will not have you wait on me
	Till I have dined my fill.
	No wife of mine, no lawful wedded wife
	Shall eat the leavings off my plate –
	That is for the children.
	I want to walk beside you in the street,
	Side by side and arm in arm
	Just like the Lagos couples I have seen
	High-heeled shoes for the lady, red paint
	On her lips. And her hair is stretched
	Like a magazine photo. I will teach you
	The waltz and we'll both learn the foxtrot
	And we'll spend the week-end in night clubs at Ibadan.
	Oh I must show you the grandeur of towns
	We'll live there if you like or merely pay visits.
	So choose. Be a modern wife, look me in the eye
	And give me a little kiss – like this.
	(kisses her.)
SIDI	(backs away.)
	No, don't! I tell you I dislike
	This strange unhealthy mouthing you perform.
	Every time, your action deceives me
	Making me think that you merely wish
	To whisper something in my ear.
	Then comes this licking of my lips with yours.
	It's so unclean. And then,
	The sound you make – 'Pyout!'
	Are you being rude to me?
LAKUNLE	(wearily.) It's never any use.
	Bush girl you are, bush girl you'll always be;
	Uncivilized and primitive – bush girl!

WOLE SOYINKA *The Lion and the Jewel*

Questions

1 What prevents Sidi from marrying Lakunle?

2 a What does Lakunle have against the custom of bride-price?
  b To what does he compare this custom?
  c Do you think he is correct?

3 From where does Lakunle get all his important-sounding words?

4 What are Lakunle's weaknesses at which Soyinka pokes fun?

5 Find evidence in the passage that tells us that Lakunle gets most of his information from print rather than from reality.

6 Describe all the ways in which Lakunle promises to treat his wife as an equal. Do you think he will carry out these promises? (Give a reason for your answer.)

7 What does Lakunle suggest is the way that 'civilized beings' eat? Do you think he is right?

8 What, in his view, does a modern wife look like?

9 What does he suggest they do in Ibadan?

10 Why does Sidi dislike being kissed?

11 What are the meanings of:
  • laughing stock
  • 'But Sidi will not make herself
    A cheap bowl for the village spit'.
  • 'Tethered, as it were, to my dirtied heels'

12 Make sentences with the following:
  • scorn
  • heritage
  • chattel

Food

The following is a conversation between the general keeper and one of the guests at a Rest House in Ghana:

'Massa, I must go to market now. I say I wan' get good meat. What you go chop?'

'I'll eat anything you cook.'

'Massa, you think you go like fried fillet of calf? Or a braised lamb liver? Yes, here a good one. An escalope of veal with onions and fried potatoes.'

'Zirigu, whom did you say you were going to cook for?'

'Yourself, Massa.'

'But that is not the food I eat.'

'But 'e be white man chop.'

'Zirigu, I no be white man. And that is the second time this morning I've told you that. And if you do it again, I'll pack up and leave.' . . .

'Massa, I beg. Don't make so. I no wan' vex you. This here chop, 'e be white man's chop. 'E be the chop I cook for all massas, for fifteen years. The Ministars, the party people, the big offisars from the army and police . . . 'E be same chop, they chop, this white man chop.'

'Zirigu, can't you cook any food of the land? Don't they sell things in that market with which you could make the food of this land?'

'Yes. But I no fit cook your kind food. No, I no fit cook food of your area.'

'How about the food of your area? Your food?'

'I no fit cook that.' . . .

'Listen Zirigu, does the Mother your wife know how to cook the food of the land?'

'Yes. But not of your area.'

'No. Of your area.'

'Yes!'

'Okay, can you charge me the normal rate for supper and ask the Mother to count my mouth in for the supper this evening?'

'W-h-a-t? What you say Massa? What?'

'I say, Zirigu, can the Mother count my stomach in for the evening's meal?'

'Massa. I no wan' play?'

'I am not playing.'

'Heh? God. You mean you go eat *tuo*?'

'Why not? At home I eat *Banku*. Isn't it the same?'

'Massa, I no wan' trouble.'

'What kind of trouble do you think you are going to get?'

'I mean your tommy.'

'What about my tummy? Do you get tummy trouble when you eat your wife's food? What are you saying, Man? And anyway, I can look after myself in that kind of way. I am a medical doctor, you know.'

'I know, young Massa. I say, this man look small but him too, 'e be big man . . . But you go chop, *tuo*?'

'Yes.'

'As for you self!'

        . . .

'S-e-t-u! S-e-t-u! S-e-t-u-e-e-e! Where is that woman? S-e-t-u!'

'What is it, Zirigu?'

'Hmmm . . . S-e-t-u . . . how shall I begin?'

'Perhaps we better wait until this evening, since I have no time to . . .'

'No . . . no . . . no! Hmm Setu, the young Master says he does not want to eat this evening.'

'And is that a story?'

'But that is not all.'

'Well, just tell me the rest.'

'He says he will eat some of your food this evening!'

'He-e-eh! Allah. Zirigu, it is not true.'

'He is in there, sitting by the table eating his orange. Go and ask him?'

'E-e-e-e Allah. Zirigu, do you think this boy is right in his head?'

'Setu, I am not sure. Setu, really, I am not sure. But his eyes do not rove so even if he is ill, it is not serious yet. He talks funny sometimes though. But I don't know. Yes, he says he will eat *tuo* and that I can charge it to his general bill. Lord, in all the twenty or so years I've been general keeper and cook for this Rest House, I have not encountered a thing like this, eh Setu, have we?'

'No, my husband. But times do change.'

'Yes, you are right, my wife. So . . . go straight to the market, buy some very good vegetables, fresh greens, okro . . .'

AMA ATA AIDOO   'For Whom Things Did Not Change'

Questions

1 What are the examples of European food that Zirigu offers the young doctor for supper?

2 Why do you think Zirigu is sure that the young man would want to eat this kind of food?

3 Zirigu is not speaking standard English to the doctor – he is speaking *pidgin*. What do you think that is, and why does he use it?

4 Do you think that it is good that a writer, like Aidoo here, uses pidgin in her stories? Why?

5 When Zirigu speaks to his wife he seems to be speaking Standard English. What is he really speaking?

6 Write out the lines that tell us that the young man is not of the same area as Zirigu.

7 What does Zirigu fear will happen if the guest eats his wife's food? Do you think he has any real cause to fear? Why?

8 Setu suggests first one and then another explanation for the doctor's unusual request. What are these two explanations and which do you think is the correct one?

9 In a previous passage it was suggested that piano and drums were symbols. Fried fillet of calf and *tuo* are also symbols in this passage. What do they symbolise?

Creative writing

It is now suppertime. Write about half a page describing the meal. What are Zirigu and Setu feeling? How does the doctor enjoy the meal? What is the reaction of the other guests to what the doctor receives on his plate?

Names – 1

Lawino is complaining about her husband Ocol's preference for Christian names:

Pagan names, he says,
Belong to sinners
Who will burn
In everlasting fires:
Ocol insists
He must be called
By his Christian name!

But my husband's name
Is so difficult to pronounce;
It sounds something like
Medikijedeki Gilirigoloyo.*

It sounds to me like
'Give the people more vegetables,
Foxes make holes in the pathway',
It sounds like a praise name
Uttered by a stammerer!
What is the meaning of 'Marta'?
Gulyelmo, Iriko, Jekcon,
Are these names of ancestors?

My Bull name is Elijy Alyeker,
I ate the name
Of the Chief of Payira,
Eliya Aliker,
Son of Awic.

Bull names are given
To chiefs of girls
Because like bulls
They lead their age-mates,
Like the full moon at night
They dominate the stars.

They are names
Of great chiefs
And great men of war.

Is 'Benedeta' a Bull name?
Is 'Maria' a Bull name
In the white man's country?

* Medikijedeki: Milchizedek
  Gilirigoloyo: Gregory

Apiyo and Acen
Are Jok names
Twins are Joks,
And are deeply respected.
Akeolo is the one
Who comes after twins,
Ajok and Ajara
Grow extra fingers or toes,
Adoc comes out
Of the belly feet first.

All these are Jok
And they are feared and respected.
When a girl is called Adong
Her father died
Just before she was born.
Akot does not mean
'Born in the rains',
But 'afterbirth
Contained bubbles of water',
And this is a sign of rain.
The daughter of
A woman with a black heart
Who kills people with poisons
Is called Akwir or Anek.

Some names are names of sorrows.
Alobo, Abur, Ayiko, Woko
That Fate has thrown
A large basket
To be filled
With dead children . . .

Who understands
The meaning of the Christian names?
The names they read for
The names of white men
That they give to children
When they put water on their heads,
What do they mean?

To me
They all sound
Like empty tins,
Old rusty tins
Thrown down
From the roof-top.

OKOT P'BITEK   *Song of Lawino*

Questions

1 Why does Ocol no longer use the name he was given at birth?

2 In the first three verses Lawino suggests two reasons why she dislikes Ocol's Christian names. What are these?

3 Why is someone given a Bull name?

4 Choose *four* examples from the many Lawino gives, of situations that give rise to names for a child. Describe these situations in your own words.

5 To what is Lawino referring in this line:
'When they put water on their heads.'

6 To what does Lawino compare the sounds of Christian names?

7 Do you think Lawino is correct in criticising Ocol's rejection of his original name? Why?

8 Do you think there is a danger in the way Lawino criticises *all* Christian names? Why?

9 Make sentences with the following words:
 • pagan
 • insists
 • stammerer
 • ancestors

10 The following comparisons are quite complicated. Can you explain them in your own words?
 . . . like bulls
 They lead their age-mates,
 Like the full moon at night
 They dominate the stars.
    and
 That Fate has thrown
 A large basket
 To be filled
 With dead children.

11 In this passage Lawino repeatedly asks questions that she does not expect to be answered. In fact she know the answers. These kinds of questions are called *rhetorical*. Write out an example of one such rhetorical question in this passage. Explain how the use of these questions adds to the effect of the poem.

Names – 2

Here are two short extracts from Petals of Blood, a novel by Ngugi wa Thiong'o.

Karega, Wanja and Abdulla are having a conversation about the significance of names:

'Karega . . . she said aloud. 'What a funny name!'

'Ritwa ni mbukio,' Karega quoted the proverb. 'Somebody a long time ago asked the question: What's in a name? And he answered that a rose would still be a rose even by another name.'

'Oh, then it would not be a rose. It would be that other name, don't you think? A rose is a rose.'

'Names are actually funny. My real name is not Abdulla. It is Murira. But I baptised myself Abdulla. Now everybody calls me Abdulla.'

'You mean, you thought Abdulla was a Christian name?' Wanja asked.

'Yes. Yes.'

They all laughed.

Questions

1 Karega gives less importance to names than Wanja does. What is the argument each of them uses? With whom do you agree?
2 Who is the 'somebody' to whom Karega refers?
3 What mistake did Abdulla make in giving himself a name?
4 Does the example of Abdulla's name lend support to Karega's or to Wanja's attitude? How?

Later Karega and Wanja talk again on this subject:

He looked back, startled by the breathing presence of another.

'It is only me,' Wanja said. 'Did I scare you?'

'No not quite. But I have a deep-seated fear of snakes, and I have always associated the poisonous things with dry plains.'

'Sssch! You should not call them by their names at night. Call them Nyamu cia Thi. I fear them too.'

'Oh, I don't believe that superstition. A leopard is called spotted one, or the shy one. Why? If their spirits can hear, they can still hear even if you call them animals of the earth or snakes or by any other name.'

'I remember that once in my hut you declared that you did not believe in names. You said something about a flower being a flower.

And she laughed a little. This slightly irritated him and he tried to explain.

'It is not that I don't believe in names. For what could be a more ridiculous caricature of self than those of our African brothers and sisters proudly calling themselves James Phillipson, Rispa, Hottensiah, Ron Rodgerson, Richard Glucose, Charity, Honey Moonsnow, Ezekiel, Shiprah, Winterbottomson – all the collection of names and non-names from the Western world? What more evidence of self-hate than their throwing a tea-party for family and friends to bribe them never to call them by their African names? It is rather that I believe in the reality of what's being named more than in the name itself.

Questions

1 Why does Wanja not wish Karega to call a snake by its name?

2 Why does Karega think that her reason is silly? Is he right? Why?

3 Again we see that Karega does not overstress the importance of names. Does this mean that he thinks it does not matter that people change their names to important-sounding European ones? Give evidence from the passage to support your answer.

4 In your own words explain what Karega thinks is more important than names. Do you agree with him? Why?

5 What is:
  • a superstition
  • a caricature
  • a non-name
  • self-hate

Further discussion

1 There seems to be an important difference in attitude between Ngugi and p'Bitek on the question of names. What is the difference and with whom do you agree? Why?

2 Is there any similarity in what these two are saying? If so, what?

3 What is the difference in the educational backgrounds of Karega and Lawino? Do you think this influences their attitudes? How?

4 What do you think is the reality behind some of the ridiculous names 'those of our African brothers and sisters' give themselves? (Remember the advent of colonialism in Africa.)

Behind the Name

Wariuki and Miriamu run away to get married after a rejection of Wariuki by Miriamu's father, Douglas Jones. Douglas Jones feels that Wariuki is too poor and unimportant to marry his daughter. Wariuki becomes obsessed (can think of nothing else) with the idea of proving Douglas Jones wrong. He slowly changes from being the happy carefree Wariuki to being the ambitious farmer and timber merchant, and senior church elder with the Christian name of Dodge W. Livingstone Jr. In the first extract part of how this change came about is described. In the second we read about Livingstone's plans for a proper Church wedding for himself and Miriamu. This he sees as a means of finally proving Douglas Jones as having been wrong about him:

(i)   It was the year of the Asian exodus. Ciana Merchants were not Kenya Citizens. Their licence would be withdrawn. They quickly offered Livingstone partnership on a fifty-fifty share basis. Praise the Lord and raise high his name. Within a year he had accumulated enough to qualify for a loan to buy one of the huge farms in Limuru previously owned by whites. He was now a big timber merchant: they made him a senior elder of the church.

Miriamu still waited for her Wariuki in vain. But she was a model wife. People praised her Christian and wifely meekness. She was devout in her own way and prayed to the Lord to rescue her from the dreams of the past. She never put on airs. She even refused to wear shoes. Every morning, she would wake early, take her Kiondo, and go to the farm where she would work in the tea estate alongside the workers. And she never forgot her old strip of land in the Old Reserve. Sometimes she made lunch and tea for the workers. This infuriated her husband: why, oh why did she choose to humiliate him before these people? Why would she not conduct herself like a Christian lady? After all had she not come from a Christian home? Need she dirty her hands now, he asked her, and with labourers too? On clothes, she gave in: she put on shoes and a white hat especially when going to Church. But work was in her bones and this she would not surrender. She enjoyed the free and open conversation with the workers.

(ii)   Cards were printed and immediately despatched. Cars and buses were lined up. He dragged Miriamu to Nairobi. They went from shop to shop all over the city: Kenyatta Avenue, Muindi Bingu Streets, Bazaar, Government Road, Kimathi Street, and back again to Kenyatta Avenue. Eventually he bought her a snow-white long-sleeved satin dress, a veil, white gloves, white shoes and stockings and of course plastic roses. He consulted Rev. Clive Schomberg's still modern classic on good manners for Africans and he hardly departed from the rules and instructions in the matrimonial sections. Dodge W. Livingstone, Jr. did not want to make a mistake.

Miriamu did not send or give invitation cards to anybody. She daily prayed that God would give her the strength to go through the whole affair. She wished that the day would come and vanish as in a dream. A week before the day, she was driven all the way back to her parents. She was a mother of two; she was no longer the young girl who once eloped; she simply felt ridiculous pretending that she was a virgin maid at her father's house. But she submitted almost as if she were driven by a power stronger than man. Maybe she was wrong, she thought. Maybe everybody else was right. Why then should she ruin the happiness of many? For even the church was very happy. He, a successful timber merchant, would set a good example to others. And many women had come to congratulate her on her present luck in such a husband. They wanted to share in her happiness. Some wept.

The day itself was bright. She could see some of the rolling fields in Molo: the view brought painful memories of her childhood. She tried to be cheerful. But attempts at smiling only brought out tears: What of the years of waiting? What of the years of hope? Her face-wrinkled father was a sight to see: a dark suit with tails, a waist-jacket, top hat and all. She inclined her head to one side, in shame. She prayed for yet more strength: she hardly recognized anybody as she was led towards the holy aisle . . .

But for Livingstone this was the supreme moment. Sweeter than vengeance. All his life he had slaved for this hour. Now it had come. He had specially dressed for the occasion: a dark suit, tails, top hat and a beaming smile at any dignitary he happened to recognize, mostly MPs, priests and businessmen. The church, Livingstone had time to note, was packed with very important people. Workers and not so important people sat outside.

Miriamu now stood before the cross: her head was hidden in the white veil. Her heart pounded. She saw in her mind's eye a grandmother pretending to be a bride with a retinue of aged bridesmaids.

NGUGI WA THIONG'O   *Wedding at the Cross*

Questions

1 Why did Ciana Merchants offer Livingstone a partnership on a fifty-fifty share basis?

2 What did he do with the money he earned?

3 What does Ngugi mean by saying that Miriamu waited for Wariuki in vain?

4 Why do you think that Livingstone hated Miriamu to cook for the workers?

5 On what issue did Miriamu give in to Livingstone?

6 What *two* things did she refuse to give in on?

7 Do you think that the issues about which she refused to listen to Livingstone were more important than those which she gave in to him about? Why?

8 Write out the sentence that tells us that Miriamu did not want to go to Nairobi.

9 Describe in your own words the preparations Livingstone makes for the wedding. Why does Ngugi write 'of course' in describing plastic roses?

10 What does Ngugi really think of Schomberg's book 'on good manners for Africans.' What is it called when a writer says the opposite of what he means? Why do writers (among other people) sometimes do this?

11 Why did Miriamu feel ridiculous at her church wedding?

12 Why did she go along with Livingstone's plans?

13 Why did she feel ashamed when she saw how her father was dressed?

14 Can you imagine why Ngugi describes Livingstone as dressed almost identically?

15 Along what lines were people segregated inside and outside the church? Describe what you imagine the difference in dress between the two groups might have been.

16 What is the meaning of the following?
  • wifely meekness
  • put on airs
  • in her bones
  • in her mind's eye

17 Find one word in the passage for each of the following:
  • the departure of a large number of people
  • collect together a large amount of something valuable
  • very religious
  • make someone very angry
  • make someone feel silly and ridiculous in front of others
  • to give in or surrender to someone else's will or control
  • a very important person

18 Now choose *five* of the words that you have found and make sentences with them.

Further discussion

Do you think Ngugi is correct in showing some connection between what was happening in Kenya economically, Livingstone's rise in wealth and the culture imitation Livingstone practiced? Why?

Creative writing

Write a short paragraph indicating how you think the story ends.

The roots of culture imitation

What follows is a description of the M.P. Nderi wa Riera:

. . . he was flooded with offers of directorships in foreign-owned companies. 'Mr Riera, you need not do anything: we do not want to take too much of your busy and valuable time. It is only that we believe in white and black partnership for real progress.' The money he had collected from his constituents for a water project was not enough for piped water. But it was adequate as a security for further loans until he bought shares in companies and invested in land, in housing and in small business. He suddenly dropped out of circulation in small places. Now he could only be found in special clubs for members only, or in newspapers – photographed while attending this or that cocktail party. As if to reinforce his new social standing, he took a huge farm in the Rift Valley. But his most lucrative connection was with the tourist industry. He owned a number of plots and premises in Mombasa, Malindi and Watamu and had been given shares in several tourist resorts all along the coast. Soon he began talking of 'the need for people to grow up and face reality. Africa needed capital and investment for real growth – not socialist slogans. But he remained a strong advocate of African culture, African personality, Black authenticity: 'If you must wear wigs, why not natural African or Black wigs?' He insisted on most of the companies of which he was chairman or director dropping their European names and taking names like Uhuru, Wananchi, Taifa, Harambee, Afro, Pan-African, which would give the enterprises a touch of the soil.

Questions

1 What is the reason that foreign companies gave to Nderi wa Riera for offering him directorships?
2 What do you imagine was the *real* reason for their offers?
3 What happened to the people's money collected for a water project?
4 Describe in your own words Nderi wa Riera's business activities.
5 What are the meanings of:
   - African personality
   - Black authenticity
   - a touch of the soil
6 Make sentences with *five* of the following:
   - constituents
   - adequate
   - invested
   - lucrative
   - capital
   - slogans
   - advocate

7 Nderi wa Riera is against the imitation of foreign culture. Write out a sentence from the passage that tells us this.

Further discussion

1 With this description of Nderi wa Riera, Ngugi seems to be pointing to the danger of drawing too much attention simply to the problems of culture imitation. We have seen that Nderi *both* cheats the people of their money for water, *and* is against culture copying. Can you describe, then, exactly what this danger is to which Ngugi is pointing?

2 Many writers, in stressing the problem of culture imitation, seem to be suggesting that a major reason for colonialism was Europe's desire to 'civilise' Africans – i.e. make them copy Western ways and customs. Do you think that this was a main cause for colonialism? Why?

Creative writing

Choose one of the themes dealt with – i.e. education or courtship or food or names, and write your own story of culture imitation.

Book list

DAVID RUBADIRI 'Stanley meets Mutesa', in Reed & Wake (eds), *A Book of African Verse,* Heinemann, 1964, pp. 68-70.

JOSÉ LUANDINO VIEIRA *The Real Life of Domingos Xavier,* Heinemann, 1978, pp. 15-16 & 67.

GABRIEL OKARA 'Piano and Drums', in Moore and Beier (eds), *Modern Poetry from Africa,* Penguin Books, 1963, pp. 121-2.

MONGO BETI *Mission to Kala,* Heinemann, 1964, p. 165.

WOLE SOYINKA 'The Lion and the Jewel', in *Collected Plays 2,* Oxford University Press, 1974, pp. 8-10.

AMA ATA AIDOO 'For Whom Things Did Not Change', in *No Sweetness Here,* Longman, 1970, pp. 16, 17, 18-19.

OKOT P' BITEK *Song of Lawino,* East African Publishing House, 1966, pp. 128-130 & 132.

NGUGI WA THIONG'O *Petals of Blood,* Heinemann, 1977, pp. 61 & 125.

NGUGI WA THIONG'O 'Wedding at the Cross', in *Secret Lives,* Heinemann, 1975, pp. 106 & 109-110.

NGUGI WA THIONG'O *Petals of Blood,* Heinemann, 1977, pp. 174-5.

Musicman   S. Hollow

Independence

The struggle for African independence from colonial powers built up in the 1950's. One of the first African colonies to gain independence was Ghana. The colonising powers were soon granting, or being forced to grant, independence to other territories. The whole industry of the struggle for independence cannot be gone into here. You will find more information about it in the references given at the end of the first chapter.

There has been a lot of disagreement as to what the gaining of independence actually meant to an ex-colony. At one extreme, some historians argue that nothing much changed. At the other, some felt that freedom was, at last, achieved. What many agree on, however, is that the imperialist powers attempted to maintain the economic structures of trade and production to enable them to continue to extract wealth from the ex-colonies. This they could do only with the assistance of a new class of Black compradors (or middlemen) whose task it was to bridge the gap between the foreign powers and the African people. By understanding this, we can begin to see what the term neo-colonialism means. One must be careful, however, not to oversimplify the situation. New classes were set into play at this time which could not be entirely or forever controlled by Europe.

Many of the writers portray some of the new Black power-holders as corrupt, abusing their power and betraying the people. It is surely somewhere within the complicated post-colonial set-up that we can seek causes for this. Unless we understand these social causes we are thrown back on explanations pointing only to fundamental human greed and selfishness.

Writers have different interpretations of what was happening at this time. What we can question is whether writers are, in fact, seeking a deeper understanding of this period of history with which they have been so preoccupied. What we also have to ask is whether it is the function or role of the writer to understand things in this way. If you think it is not, you must question why you feel this, bearing in mind that these writers have themselves chosen to write about their history and society.

Rulers

This is a rainy night.
Rulers unroll scrolls of wretched landscapes
And boast and drink and dance under chandeliers
In castles threatened like pleasure boats in a furious ocean.
They are like insects that dance around street lamps
Looming in the fog of a stormy sky.

This is a seismic night;
Water-divide hills sink into valleys
And rivers flow backwards.
Our faces and farms drip with salt water from the flooded ocean.

But while our hope splits like lips in winter
We must seek the reticent sea-gull before it drowns
Mourned by stray crows.

Such is the fate of the wicked kingdom
Governed by gorgeous parrots.

MBELLA SONNE DIPOKO   Poems of Black Africa

Questions

1 According to this poem, what do the new rulers of Africa spend most of their time doing?

2 This poem uses an extended metaphor comparing wild weather and strange, threatening happenings in the natural world to the social and political events in a newly independent country. In the *second* verse, for example, we learn that conditions in this country are comparable to a bleak time of earthquakes ('This is a seismic night;'). Nothing is happening in the correct way, which would promote life in nature or peace and prosperity in society – hills sink into valleys and rivers run backwards. It is the killing *salt* water of the sea, rather than the life-giving water of the rivers that irrigate the farms.

  a Can you show how this same extended metaphor is used in the *first* verse?

  b It is quite common in literature to compare events in nature with the social, *man-made* conditions of people and their relationships with each other as is being done here. Do you think that this comparison is appropriate (fitting) in this poem? Why?

3 Do you think the poet should use a strange and difficult word like 'seismic'? Why?

4 a The two similes in the first verse lead us to believe that these rulers may not have long in which to enjoy their power. Find evidence for this.

b   What is the effect of making each verse shorter than the one before it?
5   The sea-gull seems to be a symbol of hope. Do you think that this is effective? (Of what does a sea-gull make you think? Also, it is sea water destroying the farms. Should that influence your answer?)
6   The last two verses make use of an extended metaphor of birds. Can you explain it in your own words?
7   This poem has metaphors and/or similes in every verse. Do you think it is overloaded with them? Why?

Independence celebrations

A few days after we arrived in Kolomo Camp there was a big rally at Matero Stadium. We were told that the country was celebrating the second year of Independence. I went to the Stadium. The few times I had seen so many people in one place had been back home, when the Elephant had called the villages together to tell them about the harvesting or about Independence or about our dead heroes. There was also the time when the President had come to speak just before Independence – to ask the people to vote for him and his Party. But this day at Matero the crowd seemed to be mad with joy. The crowd frightened me a little. Their shouts and yells – *Kwacha! Kwacha! Kwacha!* – felt like a mighty wind that wanted to lift me from the ground and toss me over.

On my way back to Kolomo, in the bus, I read *Nation Times*, the evening paper. I could still hear the yells and shouts. The members of the Cabinet had been shifted from one job to another, the paper said. Asibweni – my uncle – had been made Minister of Transport and Public Works. I read aloud, 'Mr Chimba Chirundu had been Minister of Internal Affairs since Independence in 1964.' It said that the President might not have been pleased with Chirundu in Internal Affairs. The writer mentioned the event of March: the day Mrs Christine Muli, wife of Dr Muli, Minister of Education, was sent out of the country. Mr Chirundu had been forced to expel the lady. Then there were twelve African refugees in jail, locked up for being in the country without travel papers. They had been ordered out but Chirundu refused to give them papers to travel. As they could not leave, the refugees were jailed – some from Zimbabwe, from South Africa, one from Mozambique, one from Angola.

The bus stopped and jerked forward and stopped and jerked. I got off at my station. Then I stood still against an electric pole. Just as if I really needed something to lean on. Because a news item in the paper held me. I was going to read it when a bus screeched to a stop. Before I could get myself together, I realized the passengers were singing: school children from the Stadium. Earlier in the afternoon I had seen them lining the streets in the burning sun, waiting for the President and the line of government cars to pass; sleek black cars following a Rolls Royce. Then the children looked as if they might wilt in the sun. Little did I realize that I was to see this pattern repeated again and again: children drilled to stand for hours in the sun waiting for the President's motorcade to pass . . . But there in the arena again the children stood with the crowds, many with their hands on their heads, listening to hours of speech broken into by music and dance, still under the shimmering Capricorn blaze. Now in the bus, they were full of life again, as if ready for another session of dance, music and speech.

I walked on to enter the township. I remembered the item I wanted to read and stopped. Page 3: WOMAN CAUGHT IN THE COILS OF PYTHON. The story sent a cold shiver through my veins, in spite of the warm if dry air around.

ES'KIA MPHAHLELE   *Chirundu*

Questions

1 Why were there so many people at Matero Stadium?
2 Who do you think 'The Elephant' is?
3 Why did the crowd frighten the narrator?
4 What criticism of the masses of people is the narrator implying (hinting at without openly saying)? What does this also tell us about the position of the narrator himself?
5 What is one measure the President can take if he is not pleased with one of his Ministers?
6 a What is a refugee?
  b Why do you think there were refugees in this country from the countries mentioned?
7 How does the action of the buses which stop so jarringly (either jerking or screeching to a halt) add to the atmosphere the narrator is trying to create regarding the celebration of independence?
8 How do we know that the president and his government were very wealthy?
9 a What are the narrator's criticisms of the way the children are treated?
  b What does this treatment tell us regarding the independence celebrations?

10 Why do you think the narrator includes the newspaper horror story of the woman and the python. That is, what is the connection between it and the rest of the passage?

11 What are the meanings of:
- rally
- expel
- sleek
- wilt
- drilled

Portrait of a politician at home

Oyo has come with her husband to the home of the politician, Koomson, and his wife, in order to conclude a business deal:

It was amazing how much light there was in a place like this. It glinted off every object in the room. Next to each ashtray there were two shiny things: a silver box and a small toy-like pistol. The man wondered what the pistols were for. Light came off the marble tops of the little side tables. People had wondered what use a State Marble Works Corporation could be. They need not have wondered. There were uses here. . . .

'We've been having a long nap,' said Koomson, descending. 'Such a busy night, last night. We had to go to three different nightclubs.' He was in his dressing gown, a shiny thing in its own right, and he had not finished wrapping himself up in it.

'Good evening, Minister,' smiled Oyo.

'Good evening,' answered Koomson, beaming with self-esteem. Almost in the same breath, he called out: 'Atinga!' It was a peculiar kind of shout, the kind made by white men trying to pronounce African names without any particular desire to pronounce them well, indeed deriving that certain superior pleasure from their inability. The shout was answered by a loud 'Sah!' from somewhere in the back, and in a moment a thin, short man, about fifty, stood at the back door, awaiting his master's instructions. . . .

Mrs Koomson descended the stairs, wearing a dress that seemed to catch each individual ray of light and aim it straight into the beholding eye. She, like her husband, did not take a drink. She sat languidly in her chair, and for some time she did nothing but stroke her wig from front to back in motions that were long, slow, and very studied.

AYI KWEI ARMAH   *The Beautyful Ones Are Not Yet Born*

49

Questions

1 What are the 'silver box' and 'small toy-like pistol'? Why are there so many in the room?

2 Why is the writer critical of a State Marble Works Corporation in a developing country? What reason is he suggesting for the existence of such enterprises?

3 How do we know that the writer feels that politicians like Koomson spend very little, if any, time working for their country?

4 What is the meaning of 'self-esteem', and why is Koomson so full of it?

5 Why does Koomson address his servant as though he cannot pronounce his name?

6 Why do you think that we are told that the servant is 'about fifty'?

7 The main character in this novel is, in fact, Oyo's husband and he is referred to only as 'the man' (i.e. not by name).

   a How do we know that the man and his wife move in entirely different social circles from the Koomsons?

   b Find evidence in the passage for the fact that the Koomsons feel superior to their guests.

   c Can you guess a reason as to why the main character remains nameless?

8 What is meant by the comment that Mrs Koomson's motions were 'very studied'?

9 a What do the description of the room, Koomson, and his wife all have in common?

   b Why are they all described in this way?

10 Make sentences with:
- peculiar
- deriving
- languidly

Further discussion

1 A *caricature* is an exaggerated (overdone) portrait of a type of character. It is used to criticise real weaknesses thought to be in that type of person. Because it is so overdone, this sort of portrayal often makes us laugh.

   a In what ways can we say that many African writers caricature the new rulers of independent Africa?

   b There is a danger that the caricature can be used *in place of* any serious explanation for the social situation in a neo-colony. Do you think that this has been the case in the foregoing passages, or in any other works you may have read? Why?

Creative writing

Write your own caricature of someone. Try to see the person as a particular 'type' and exaggerate their mannerisms, habits, expressions and so on.

Let us now look at the following three passages which are beginning to ask important questions about the situation in newly independent African countries.

The Accident

Towards the beginning of the rainy season, he accompanied his grandmother to her lands which were some twenty miles outside the village. They sowed seed together after the hired tractor had turned up the land but the boy's main chore was to keep the household pot filled with meat. Sometimes they ate birds Friedman had trapped, sometimes they ate fried tortoise-meat or wild rabbit; but there was always something as the bush abounded with animal life. Sejosenye only had to take a bag of mealie meal, packets of sugar, tea, and powdered milk as provisions for their stay at the lands; meat was never a problem. Mid-way through the ploughing season, she began to run out of sugar, tea and milk.

'Friedman,' she said that evening. 'I shall wake you early tomorrow morning. You will have to take the bicycle into the village and purchase some more sugar, tea, and milk.'

He was up at dawn with the birds, a solitary figure cycling on a pathway through the empty bush. By nine, he had reached the village and first made his way to Ga-Sefete-Molemo ward and the yard of a friend of his grandmother, who gave him a cup of tea and a plate of porridge. Then he put one foot on the bicycle and turned to smile at the woman with his beautiful gazelle eyes. His smile was to linger vividly before her for many days as a short while later, hard pounding feet came running into her yard to report that Friedman was dead.

He pushed the bicycle through the winding, sandy pathway of the village ward, reached the high embankment of the main road, peddled vigorously up it and out of the corner of his eye, saw a small green truck speeding towards him. In the devil-may-care fashion of all the small boys, he cycled right into its path, turned his head and smiled appealingly at the driver. The truck caught him on the front bumper, squashed the bicycle and dragged the boy along at a crazy speed for another hundred yards, dropped him and careered on another twenty yards before coming to a halt. . . .

The people of Ga-Sefete-Molemo ward buried the boy Friedman but none of them would go near the hospital where Sejosenye lay. The stories brought to them by way of the nurses were too terrible for words. They said the old woman sang and laughed and talked to herself all the time. So they merely asked each other: 'Have you been to see Mma-Sejosenye?' 'I'm afraid I cannot. It would kill my heart.' Two weeks later, they buried her.

As was village habit, the incident was discussed thoroughly from all sides till it was understood. In this timeless, sleepy village, the goats stood and suckled their young ones on the main road or lay down and took their afternoon naps there. The motorists either stopped for them or gave way. But it appeared that the driver of the truck had neither brakes on his car nor a driving licence. He belonged to the new rich civil-servant class whose salaries had become fantastically high since independence. They had to have cars in keeping with their new status; they had to have any car, as long as it was a car; they were in such a hurry about everything that they couldn't be bothered to take driving lessons. And thus progress, development, and a pre-occupation with status and living standards first announced themselves to the village. It looked like being an ugly story with many decapitated bodies on the main road.

BESSIE HEAD   'The Wind and a Boy', from *The Collector of Treasures*

Questions

1 In what ways did Friedman help his grandmother at the lands?
2 Why was a bicycle very useful to have at the lands?
3 Describe in your own words how the accident happened.
4 What were the effects of Friedman's death on his grandmother?
5 Why did no-one visit Sejosenye in hospital?
6 Describe in your own words the new class to which the driver of the truck belonged and the writer's criticism of it.
7 Bessie Head is suggesting that the accident was not just a freak, isolated event, like, for example, an earthquake, but the result of historical developments in this African country (Botswana).
   a What are these developments that she very briefly describes in this story?
   b Is it effective for a writer to use the sad story of a boy and his death to highlight (describe, explain) these developments? Why?
8 In what way is the writer being ironic in this sentence: 'And thus progress, development, and a preoccupation with status and living-standards first announced themselves to the village'?
9 Write out a sentence that tells us that the writer is not very hopeful about the future.
10 What is the effect of the phrase 'hard pounding feet' to describe the messenger who reported Friedman's death?

52

11 Make sentences with *five* of the following:
- abounded
- provisions
- solitary
- vigorously
- careered
- status
- pre-occupation
- decapitated

Here are two passages from a novel called Violence *about the different opportunities that the workers and the wealthy have of making money in independent Nigeria:*

How to earn money

(i) . . . a tipper (truck) had drawn up and he had become involved in a great struggle with the other labourers to get as near to the tipper as he could. He saw himself struggling, fighting, cursing and sweating and anxious, and his mind grew more bitter. How could he go back to all these things, to the overpowering heat of the sun, to the numbness of hunger, to the despair of returning home each evening after a day's long wait? How? What alternatives had he? And what hadn't he done to earn money? He had even sold his blood to make money. Yes, given out pints of his blood for as little as fifteen naira a pint. Sold his blood so that he and Adisa would not starve, so that they could survive. And this he had done not once nor twice but many times. Always, the men who wanted the blood came to them at Iyaro in their big long cars. Always, they were hesitant to say they wanted to buy the blood.

'We want some . . .' and the men would hesitate, looking at the hard set faces of the labourers. But the labourers understood, always.

Always, after they had decided to sell their blood, they would stand in the shadow of the water tower, away from the main body of the other labourers and as they waited, their faces hard and set, they would be hungry, frustrated and silent. Always.

The last time he and Osaro had gone to sell their blood, it had been to a man in a big Mercedes Benz car. The car had drawn up close to where they were standing and in the car were the driver, the man and a boy. The man and the boy sat at the back of the car and then the man had rolled down the window glass and beckoned to them.

He saw it again clearly now, very very clearly, the man, the boy and himself and then the hospital. . . .

(ii) Inside the Freedom Motel, cutlery and teeth clattered as they bit and chewed, tongues wagged as the beer and the palm wine were swallowed and gulped down. In one corner a group of customers talked about the prices, prices higher than the tallest buildings in the city, frightful prices. They thought and talked about money, how to steal to make money, cheat to make money, work to make money, make money to make money. They talked and concluded that the best way to make money was to steal it from the government. Steal a huge sum, put most of it in some foreign bank, make business with the government's money, steal goods and equipment ordered by the government, steal government cement on the high seas, steal land and buildings from the people in the name of the government. Yes, steal, cheat, dupe and even murder in the name of the government. They talked and concluded that the government encouraged stealing, applauded and rewarded it. What was retirement with full benefits, they asked? Steal. Steal huge, gigantic sums, hundreds of thousands, hundreds of millions of naira of government money and be retired with full applause. Steal and be retired and then enter business.

They talked and plotted ways of stealing. Then they laughed and kept quiet and listened to the loud music coming from a player in another corner of the motel. The music was sharp and flat but these customers listened and tapped their fingers on their knees and shuffled their feet on the floor in response to the sharp shrilling and flat music that came from the corner of the motel.

FESTUS IYAYI *Violence*

Questions

1 Write out the words that tell us that there was great competition betwen the unemployed labourers to find work.

2 Why did Idemudia (the main character) sell his blood?

3 How do we know that the people who bought the blood were very wealthy?

4 If the man and the boy sat at the back of the car, who do you think drove it?

5 The wealthy are buying blood for their sick relatives in hospital.

   a What does this tell us about the hospital system in this country?

   b What do you think happened to *poor* people who were sick and needed blood?

6 What is the effect of the repetition of the word 'always' in the first passage?

7 The labourers often did *in reality* sell their blood to the wealthy.

   a In what way, however, can one also say that this practice was *symbolic* of the relationship between the rich and the poor?

   b Do you think it is an effective symbol? Why?

8 What is the *irony* in the name of the motel?

9 Pick out the words that tell us that the writer is disgusted by the way the customers gossip and eat and drink so greedily.

10 Describe in some detail and in your own words why they concluded that the best way to make money *and* get away with it, was to steal from the government.

11 Who, in fact, is being robbed when these people steal in the name of the government?

12 What is the effect of the description of the music as 'sharp shrilling and flat'?

Further discussion

1 The second passage does not tell us from where the government gets these huge sums of money. Where do you think it comes from?

2 Compare and contrast these two passages from *Violence*. In both, the question of how to make money is asked. Why are the answers so different? What is the difference in tone (mood) between the two passages? Is this kind of contrast effective? Why?

Uhuru

The following passage is about a group of University students during the period of Independence coming to East Africa:

I went back to my studies and prepared for the coming exams. Most of us got through and were accepted in Makerere, then the only University College in East Africa . . . no – not quite true . . . there was Dar es Salaam . . . but then it had only started. No more fees. No more rules and restrictions. We wore worsted gaberdines and smoked and danced. We even had pocket money. Uhuru also came to our countries. We sang and danced and wept. Tomorrow. Cha. Cha. Cha. Uhuru. Cha. Cha. Cha. We streamed into the streets of Kampala. We linked hands and chanted: Uhuru. Cha. Cha. Cha. It was a kind of collective madness, I remember . . . The story was the same for each of us. But none of us I am quite sure that night fully realized the full import of what had happened. This we knew in the coming years and perhaps Wahinya had been right. And what years, my Lord! Strange things we heard and saw: most of those who had finished Makerere were now being trained as District Officers, Labour Officers, Diplomats, Foreign Service – all European jobs. Uhuru. Cha. Cha. Cha. Others were now on the boards of Shell, Caltex, Esso, and other oil companies. We could hardly wait for our turn. Uhuru. Cha. Cha. Cha. Some came for the delayed graduation ceremonies. They came in their dark suits, their cars and red-lipped ladies in heels. They talked of their jobs, of their cars, of their employees; of their mahogany-furnished offices and of course their European and Asian secretaries. So this was true. No longer the rumours, no longer the unbelievable stories. And we were next in the queue.

We now dreamt not of sweets, Fanta and ginger-ale. The car was now our world. We compared names: VW, DKW, Ford Prefects, Peugeots, Flying A's. Mercedes Benzes were then beyond the reach of our imagination. Nevertheless, it all seemed a wonder that we would soon be living in European mansions, eat in European hotels, holiday in European resorts at the coast and play golf. And with such prospects before my eyes, how could I remember Wahinya?

NGUGI WA THIONG'O   'A Mercedes Funeral' from *Secret Lives*

Questions

1 a How do we know that there were very few University graduates relative to the total population of Kenya?

  b What could be a collective noun (name) for this small group of privileged people?

2 Who do you think now paid their fees and pocket money?

3 What do you think *Uhuru* means?

4 What is the purpose of repeating the words 'Uhuru' and 'Cha Cha Cha' – i.e. what is the writer trying to tell us about the meaning of Uhuru for these university graduates?

5 What is the meaning of a 'collective madness'?

6 How do we know that a University degree guaranteed top jobs for the graduates?

7 Write out a line that tells us that these graduates had not really come from very wealthy homes.

8 In your own words describe in what ways, according to this writer, Uhuru changed very little in Kenya.

9 Describe in detail evidence in the passage that the new Kenyan rulers were concerned only with obtaining benefits for themselves and not with developing their country.

10 We are not told much about Wahinya in this passage. (You will have to read the story to find out more about him.) How do we know, however, that his and the narrator's lives take quite different paths?

11 Explain the metaphor 'And we were next in the queue'.

Further discussion

1 Think about the last three passages and discuss these questions:
   a What do they share in common, and in what ways are they different?
   b Which did you enjoy most and why?
   c Would you agree that they teach us the danger of looking at this period of African history in strictly *racial* terms? How?

The above three passages are still fairly indirect in their comments about the social situation in some post-independent African countries. The following two passages, on the other hand, are very explicit (open, direct) in their analysis of this situation.

Africanisation

BUSINESSMAN, *a well-dressed portly fellow, and* BANKER, *an executive type white man, enter.*

BANKER   As I was saying, Mr Mafutha, I am going to back you all the way for the chairmanship of the Stock Exchange.

BUSINESSMAN   That is very kind of you, sir, I, too, am going to put hard work into it to show that I am worth the office.

BANKER   You are worth it, Mr Mafutha. I tell you. You are worth it.

BUSINESSMAN   And with your backing I am sure of success.

BANKER   Why, of course. I tell you man, all the white businessmen will support you. I made them come to their senses at last. I don't have to tell you all this, but it had come to a stage where I had to theaten not to give them any more loans and overdrafts. That brought them to their senses.

BUSINESSMAN   Our country is blessed with bank managers like you. You don't think the white concerns will cause trouble for me when I take up the chairmanship?

BANKER   You won't give them a chance, man. If you do your job well how can they cause trouble for you? The only thing you have to do is to listen to our advice. I met your Ministers about this. They too are quite clear about this. They know that without us they wouldn't be where they are now. All this opposition to your taking up the chairmanship is based on mistrust. No African has ever been chairman of the Stock Exchange in this country, you know. And you have been independent for the last ten years.

BUSINESSMAN	Africanisation seems to be failing when it comes to commerce and industry, eh. Look at the Chamber of Commerce – it's all in the hands of the Twiddles and their friends.
BANKER	What do you expect, my friend. All big business is in foreign hands. Foreign investment, you know. Surely in the interest of the huge sums these people have invested in your country one should expect some little mistrust – especially as we have so far never had an African wielding power in the Stock Exchange. Self protection is instinctive, man, and one can't blame the white concerns. To them it doesn't matter a hoot that your being the chairman will not affect the stocks and shares one way or the other.
BUSINESSMAN	You are right, sir.
BANKER	That is why I say you must prove them wrong. You must show them that their fears are groundless. You are the emerging capitalist in the emergent Africa. That is one more reason why you should succeed. To teach our incompetent socialist neighbours the art of running the economy of a state without making a mess of it all.

As they pass the hoboes' bench JANABARI looks at BANKER and BUSINESSMAN with what he thinks is a friendly grin.

JANABARI	Good morning, sir, Mr Mafutha.
SERGEANT	How are you, Mr Mafutha?

BUSINESSMAN looks the other way and walks on with offended pomposity. BANKER smiles condescendingly at the hoboes, but their eyes follow BUSINESSMAN as he walks on.

BUSINESSMAN and BANKER go out.

JANABARI	Mh, Serge, it is our people who snub us.
SERGEANT	I don't think he was trying to snub us really. You can see that he is busy with the banker. Perhaps negotiating an overdraft. You shouldn't have greeted him so stupidly. He is a big man, you know.
JANABARI	But he has always snubbed us, Serge. And you always have an excuse for him. Yesterday he was late for a meeting of the board of directors. Last week he was hurrying for an appointment at the American Embassy. Serge, wonder how you know all these things.
SERGEANT	Commonsense, my friend. A businessman is always busy.
JANABARI	Do we have anything on him in our files?
SERGEANT	Mmh. . . Mr Mafutha. Wait, let's see. (*Looks at his notebook*) Yes. He lives in the new suburbs. His house is at the corner of Freedom Road and Constitution Street.
JANABARI	Aha! He is the fellow who was in hospital for the whole of last month.
SERGEANT	Eke, my training is showing some results, eh. You know something about everybody. For sure that is the man.

	Suffered from some of these ailments we hear so much about these days.
JANABARI	Some of these upper-class ailments.
SERGEANT	Was it not something like high blood-pressure?
JANABARI	Psha! High blood-pressure. That's too commonplace, Serge. Gone are the days when high blood-pressure used to be the privilege soley of the higher class. It gets everybody these days. Peasants and all.
SERGEANT	What was it then, Janabari?
JANABARI	I don't remember, but it was real sophisticated stuff. Something like gastric ulcers or some such new-fangled disease.
SERGEANT	What is he worth, Janie?
JANABARI	You mean you don't have that in the book?
SERGEANT	Your oversight, I am sure. You never gave me that information or else I would have written it.
JANABARI	They say he is worth a million. He is in all the big companies. White companies too.
SERGEANT	Would there be any wisdom if we turned corner Freedom Road and Constitution Street into our operational area sometime next week?

ZAKES MDA   *We Shall Sing For The Fatherland*

Questions

1 How long has this unamed African country been independent?

2 What finally made the White businessmen agree to support Mr Mafutha as chairman of the Stock Exchange?

3 Find evidence in the passage for the fact that Mr Mafutha will not really be able to make his own decisions in this job. That is, who is shown to hold the real power in the country?

4 Why then do you think that the banker wants a *black* man to hold this important position, at least in name? (In your answer consider both people like the hoboes who helped fight for independence and also the 'socialist neighbours' that the banker refers to.)

5 What do you think the fears of the 'white concerns' are, and why does the banker think they are groundless?

6 Do you agree that 'self-protection is instinctive'? Why?

7 Why do you think Mr Mafutha snubs the hoboes, Janabari and Sergeant?

8 Why was Mr Mafutha in hospital for a month?

9 Why do the hoboes keep 'files' and what do you think they mean by their 'operational area'?

10 What do you think Mr Mafutha does in all the big white companies?

11 What are the meanings of:
- overdrafts
- Africanisation
- Foreign investment
- offended pomposity

12 a Find one word in the passage that means each of the following:
- large, quite fat
- resistance, hostility to
- looking down on someone, behaving towards someone in a superior manner
- arranging a business affair
- that which is obvious if you think carefully about it
- that which has been left out or not seen to by mistake

b Now choose *three* of the words you have found and make sentences with them.

Creative writing

It is night time. Sergeant and Janabari are circling Mr Mafutha's house looking for a way in . . .
Continue the story.

The New Ilmorog

Indeed, changes did come to Ilmorog, changes that drove the old one away and ushered a new era in our lives. And nobody could tell, really tell, how it had happened, except that it had happened. Within a year or so of the New Ilmorog shopping centre being completed, wheatfields and ranches had sprung up all around the plains: the herdsmen had died or had been driven further afield into the drier parts, but a few had become workers on the wheatfields and ranches on the earth upon which they once roamed freely. The new owners, master-servants of bank power, money and cunning, came over at weekends and drove in Landrovers or Range Rovers, depending on the current car fashion, around the farms whose running they had otherwise entrusted to paid managers. The peasants of Ilmorog had also changed. Some had somehow survived the onslaught. They could employ one or two hands on their small farms. Most of the others had joined the army of workers who had added to the growing population of the New Ilmorog. But which New Ilmorog?

There were several Ilmorogs. One was the residential area of the farm managers, County Council officials, public service officers, the managers of Barclays, Standard and African Economic Banks, and other servants of state and money power. This was called Cape Town. The other – called New Jerusalem – was a shanty town of migrant and floating workers, the unemployed, the prostitutes and small traders in tin and scrap metal. . . .

The shopping and business centre was dominated by two features. Just outside it was a tourist cultural (Utamaduni) village owned by Nderi wa Riera and a West German concern, appropriately called Ilmorog African Diamond Cultural and Educational Tours. . . . The other was Theng'eta Breweries which, starting on the premises owned by Mzigo, had now grown into a huge factory employing six hundred workers with a number of research scientists and chemical engineers. . . .

The breweries were owned by an Anglo-American international combine but of course with African directors and even shareholders. Three of the four leading local personalities were Mzigo, Chui and Kimeria.

Long live New Ilmorog! Long live Partnership in Trade and Progress!

NGUGI WA THIONG'O *Petals of Blood*

Questions

1 Who owned the new wheatfields and ranches?

2 Write out the words in the passage that tell us that private ownership of this land was something new.

3 How do we know that the new owners did not live on their land? Who ran the farms for them?

4 On what basis did these people choose which cars they bought?

5 What happened to the peasants of Ilmorog?

6 Describe in your own words three different New Ilmorogs portrayed by the writer.

7 Why was the name of the tourist cultural village 'appropriate'?

8 Who were the power-holders in the Theng'eta breweries?

9 In what way is the writer being *ironic* at the end of the passage?

10 *A paradox* is a seemingly absurd, impossible and even contradictory statement that, on second glance, contains a lot of truth in it. In what way is the description of the new owners as 'master-servants of bank power' a paradox?

11 Explain the metaphor 'army of workers'.

12 What are 'migrant and floating workers'?

Further discussion

1 Compare the last two passages with the three that went before them. The former are quite obviously much more direct and explicit in their criticism of some post-independent African countries.

   a Can you think of any other differences and/or similarities between them?

   b Do you think that literature has a right to be so explicit and to try to teach us about history and society; or do you feel it should be only entertaining and/or beautiful?

   c Do you think that these last two passages are well written? Do you think their style has suffered because they are so direct and explicit? If so, do you think that this is inevitable (unavoidable)?

Book list

MBELLA SONNE DIPOKO   'Rulers' in Soyinka, (ed.), *Poems of Black Africa*, Heinemann, 1975, p. 115.

ES'KIA MPHAHLELE   *Chirundu*, Raven press, 1979, pp. 113 – 4.

AYI KWEI ARMAH   *The Beautyful Ones are Not Yet Born*, Heinemann, 1969, pp. 171, 172, 173 & 174.

BESSIE HEAD   'The Wind and a Boy', in *The Collector of Treasures*, Heinemann, 1977, pp. 74 – 5.

FESTUS IYAYI   *Violence*, Longman, 1979, pp. 161 – 2 & 289 – 90.

NGUGI WA THIONG'O   'A Mercedes Funeral' in *Secret Lives*, Heinemann, 1975, pp. 126 – 7.

ZAKES MDA   *We shall Sing For the Fatherland*, Raven, 1972, pp. 13 – 15.

NGUGI WA THIONG'O   *Petals of Blood*, Heinemann, 1977, pp. 280 – 1.

Drum and horn   S. Hollow

The Future

Speculation about the future is, of course, a tricky and dangerous exercise. Nonetheless, we all do it and African writers are no exception. There are many different views to be found in the writing. It is hoped that the following passages capture the most popular of these views. Perhaps the most common type of vision for the future presented by African literature is to be found in the first passage. This does not necessarily mean that it is the most reliable.

Here history is seen as endlessly repeating itself – hence 'nothing changes'. The next passage sees change as happening only through the work of an elite, a small group of those supposed to be the best, most talented people in the society. The last two passages suggest that it is the majority of people, the ordinary workers and peasants, who are the hope for the future.

Throughout the chapter you will be asked what you think about when considering the future of Africa.

Nothing Changes

The narrator is a lawyer from Ghana who becomes disappointed (disillusioned) with the political situation in his country:

At a Party rally the other day, a man led the gathering in prayer for prosperity, long life for the Leader, safety for all, and proceeded to compile a list, with the help of Party activists from corporations of those who are known to be anti-Party, and must be detained so that the Party and Leader must remain forever. Then they sang a hymn, 'Lead Kindly Light Amidst the Encircling Gloom, Lead Thou Me on'. This was ended with the Party anthem, 'There is Victory for Us'.

Three days after, the anti-Party elements were flung into the maximum security prison in Nsawam.

After the firing of the muskets on the famous twenty-fourth, the Party activists were rounded up. Some were screaming in tears and supplication, some marched with their heads bowed. Then they were beaten, on television only. They were not beaten in reality. The world was told it was a bloodless take-over. Some women have not seen their husbands since, except those who saw their husbands since in Army uniforms driving Mercedes 250 top speed towards the Castle. The same Castle where the slaveships anchored, and received their cargoes through the tunnels to the Americas.

On the Liberty Arch the words are inscribed, 'Freedom and Justice'. The darkness of the black star lies in its square where immense appropriations are made to increase the striking force of the army of a starving, naked and diseased nation to march and wear its boots newly received from England under certificates of urgency – judging the state of depletion of the national coffers – the one who left stole all the money . . . – new epaulettes, new strings, new crowns for newly appointed generals and brigadiers, and uniforms for latrine carriers. . . .

Nkrumah, from all accounts, just continued the work of the British colonialists. Government by force of arms – vis et armis – Government by chicanery, tricks, new tricks will be worked out with devastating logic for a one-party state in which colonial activists will attend a meeting where they will collect a guinea per head to build a writers' and artists' home at the beach – between the lagoon and the sea in the picturesque village of Botianor. Lectures will have to be organised to explain the African personality, the role of the press, and the importance of creating a new identity, after centuries of colonial rule, slavery and rape. The rape of a continent in darkness.

KOFI AWOONOR   *This Earth, My Brother . . .*

Questions

1 What happened to those who opposed the Party?

2 a In what way is the writer being *ironic* when he refers to the hymn singing and the titles of the Hymn and the Party anthem?
  b When he describes uniforms for latrine carriers or a writers' and artists' beach home, the writer is really saying the same thing. What is he saying and how is he being ironic here?
  c Can you find another example of irony in the passage?
  d The writer uses a lot of irony in this passage. Do you think this is effective? Why?

3 What happend to 'The Party activists' themselves?

4 Why are we suspicious that what was told to the world and what happened in reality are two different things?

5 a Why do you think the writer makes a reference to the slave castle? (Think carefully about your answer to this question.)
  b How do we know that the writer feels that there is, in fact, little chance of creating a new identity 'after centuries of colonial rule, slavery and rape'?

6 Find evidence in the passage that the writer is disgusted by the fact that money is spent on equipping the army while the people are starving.

7 What do you imagine 'the black star' symbolises?

8 The writer has some important criticisms to make of Nkrumah. What are these? (Read through the whole passage for your answer.)

9 What do seven of the following phrases mean?:
  • a Party rally
  • Party activists
  • bloodless take-over
  • the striking force of the army
  • certificates of urgency
  • government of chicanery
  • one-party state
  • African personality
  • The rape of a continent in darkness.

10 Find one word in the passage that means:
  • kept in prison
  • begging for mercy
  • huge, enormous
  • money set aside
  • toilet
  • having terrible consequences or results
  • pretty place

Only the Few Seek Change

Ofeyi and the other character are plotting the assassination of some of the evil and corrupt people of power in an African country.

Ofeyi watched, admiring his nerve. Except for details of scruple, he found himself increasingly accepting the fact that they were kindred spirits. A rage engulfed him at his imprisonment within the dilemma, an exaggeration of the mere part against the whole. There was something a little unnatural in this process of resolving the ethics of assassination, preparing oneself to accept or reject the cold-blooded necessity with a minimum of feeling. Demanding in return only the residual sensation of the freed conscience exhilarated, a dreamless sleep, the knowledge that one has taken decision on behalf of the guiltless inmates of overcrowded prisons, of innocents disembowelled on the points of stakes, shot in the silence of their homes, pauperized and degraded by a totalitarian maul, brained by leprous accretions that even devoured their own fingers in the reckless pace of gluttony.

If it were possible – yes, that was the grim temptation – if it were possible to ignore even the unformed, irrational whisper, the purely psychic intuition to succumb to the peace of amnesia, expunge all knowledge and define freedom as the freedom not to listen; to read ony the official newspapers, to avoid conversations refuse to open letters whose origins could not be immediately identified and thus to evade the cry of distant suppliants . . .

It seemed that few enough hands sought the sluice gates of light and life, of truly making grow, turning moist and live . . .

Droused by the hum of the engine a sensation close to what he had experienced in Iriyise's room came over him, that of being alone in the world. Only this time, he saw where the rest of mankind had rushed, and now his was the only consciousness observing the dark pulsating chasms of tearing, grasping, clawing, gorging humanity.

WOLE SOYINKA *Season of Anomy*

Questions

1 Write out a line that tells us that Ofeyi is agonizing over the decision to assassinate these people.

2 What is the difference between himself and the other character referred to at the beginning of the passage?

3 a What does the writer see as the benefits of having taken such a decision on behalf of the people?

  b How do we know that the writer does not think much of humanity in general and of the people's ability to bring about change for themselves?

c Pick out the metaphor that is used to describe the very few who seek change. Explain this metaphor in your own words.

d What do you think of the writer's attitude here? Why?

4 Why do you think that the inmates of the prisons are described as 'guiltless'?

5 Describe in your own words some of the dreadful things that have happened to people in this country.

6 Pick out and explain a metaphor used by the writer to describe the terrible greed (gluttony) of some of the power-holders.

7 What are the meanings of:
  - kindred spirits
  - dilemma
  - cold-blooded necessity
  - exhilarated
  - cry of distant suppliants

8 This passage uses quite a lot of difficult words. Do you think it is well written? Why?

9 Choose four words from this passage that you think are useful (expressive, have a nice sound to them etc.) Make a sentence with each of them so as to illustrate their meanings.

Further discussion

The writers of this and the previous passage are very *pessimistic*. What is the meaning of this word? Compare and contrast what these passages have to say in terms of their pessimism.

Creative writing

Both passages discussed in this section so far refer to the difference between official newspaper reports and reality. Make up an incident of your own and write it up first as the report in one such official newspaper, then as a description of what really happened. Both accounts should be quite short.

Chaiba the Algerian

There seemed to be no flesh on his body, and the skin was stretched tight over the bones of his face; his thin-lipped mouth had deep lines on either side, and his hair had receded from his narrow forehead. But he had mischievous, laughing eyes, dark grey, with thick lashes and eyebrows. His colour was not the dark tan that racialists usually associate with all North African Arabs, but was more like the subdued shade that the African soil takes on at twilight and at dawn . . .

He came from the Aurès, the mountainous region south of Constantine, but he rarely talked about his native village or his homeland. His wife and children had joined him. He liked some aspects of France but had a deep hatred of the caids and the colonists. I never discovered why, however. He liked his snuff; when he took a pinch, his eyes twinkled under their long lashes. A favourite subject of his was the cinema. On Sundays he took his whole family to see a film. He always went to the same cinema, in the rue des Dominicaines. It was the only one where Arab films were shown. Afterwards, they all went back home to a furnished room.

He worked hard, doing overtime to send some money to help his relatives in Algeria. We were walking home at six o'clock one morning, at the end of a sixteen-hour shift. Another docker, a European, was with us. Just as we reached the Colbert post office, a police patrol on bicycles stopped us. After checking our identity-cards, they took Chaiba away with them. He was detained for three days. Why? From that time, never a week passed without the police questioning him. As if some disease were eating him away, gradually rotting his whole body, Chaiba became increasingly morose and hardly ever spoke a word. He stopped going to the cinema with his family.

A few days ago, while in Dakar, I saw in a newspaper that Chaiba had been deported, had been put in an internment camp, had tried to escape while armed with a weapon, and been shot dead.

The Algerian War of Independence had been on for six years. I never knew what Chaiba's ideas and feelings were on that subject. He was fully entitled to hate caids and colonists if he wished. He was not an extremist and certainly not a revolutionary. But he had been born in Algeria. His colour was that of the African soil at twilight. He loved his wife and children, went to the cinema once a week to see Arab films, liked his snuff . . . All that did not make a revolutionary of him.

But perhaps he believed that dignity and the respect of his children could only be acquired at the cost of a certain kind of life.

Chaiba was a friend. I am proud to think that he was a friend with his colour like that of the African soil at dawn – a new dawn for Africa.

SEMBENE OUSMANE   'Chaiba the Algerian', from Tribal Scars

Questions

1 Describe Chaiba's appearance in your own words.
2 What job did Chaiba do?
3 How do we know that he did not have much leisure time?
4 How does the writer build up a picture of Chaiba as just an ordinary working man and 'not an extremist and certainly not a revolutionary'?
5 In what conflict raging in Africa was Chaiba caught up?
6 Describe in your own words events leading up to the shooting of Chaiba.

7 What kind of life is the writer referring to as having to be sacrificed in order for Chaiba to win the respect of his children?

8 What was the relationship between Chaiba and the writer?

9 Explain the simile 'As if some disease were eating him away, gradually rotting his whole body, Chaiba became increasingly morose . . .'

10 a Explain this simile repeated in the passage: 'his colour like that of the African soil at dawn'.

   b In what way is his skin colour used as a *symbol of hope* in the future of Africa?

11 Make sentences with *five* of the following:
   - racialists
   - subdued
   - detained
   - morose
   - deported
   - entitled
   - dignity

Creative writing

There are not many examples in literature where an ordinary working person is the hero. This short sketch of Chaiba by Sembene is one of the few that we find. Imagine such a character of your own and write a description of him or her.

A Human Kingdom

The true lesson of history was this: that the so-called victims, the poor, the downtrodden, the masses, had always struggled with spears and arrows, with their hands and songs of courage and hope, to end their oppression and exploitation: that they would continue struggling until a human kingdom came: a world in which goodness and beauty and strength and courage would be seen not in how cunning one can be, not in how much power to oppress one possessed, but only in one's contribution in creating a more human world in which the inherited inventive genius of man in culture and science from all ages and climes would be not the monopoly of a few, but for the use of all, so that all flowers in all their different colours would ripen and bear fruits and seeds. And the seeds would be put into the ground and they would once again sprout and flower in rain and sunshine. If Abdulla could choose a brother, why couldn't they all do the same? Choose brothers and sisters in sweat, in toil, in struggle, and stand by one another and strive for that kingdom?. . .

He now knew his line of attack and approach. *These divisions had to end* if they were going to successfully demand recognition and a fair share of their own sweat. From nowhere, so it seemed, pamphlets started appearing: and they all carried the same theme: workers were all children of the machine and the New Road. Those who owned the machine did not care where a worker came from in the game of exploitation. But the machine and the New Road were the children of the workers, for it was their sweat that built the road, the factory, and it was they who sustained the whole complex by their energy and consumption. The machine was no less their father than they were its father, and the struggle in future would be fought on who should own and control the machine and the products: those whose sweat made it move or those whose power was the bank, and who came to reap and harvest where they had not ploughed or planted. Every dispute was put in the context of the exploitation of labour by capital, itself stolen from other workers. Why should so few wield power of life and death over so many?

NGUGI WA THIONG'O   *Petals of Blood*

Questions

1 Why does Ngugi refer to 'the *so-called* victims' – i.e. why does he refuse himself to see 'the downtrodden' simply as poor victims?
2 In your own words summarise the narrator's vision of 'a human kingdom'.
3 a Explain the extended metaphor (a metaphor that is worked on and developed) 'so that all flowers in all their different colours would ripen and bear fruits and seeds. And the seeds would be put into the ground and they would once again sprout and flower in rain and sunshine.'
   b This metaphor is in direct contrast with the one that forms the title of the novel – i.e. 'Petals of Blood'. What do you imagine the latter means?
4 What divisions do you think Ngugi is referring to? (See words in italics.)
5 What is meant by 'a fair share of their own sweat'?
6 Why does the narrator feel that the machine and the New Road should be controlled by the workers and not by those who owned the machine? (Read carefully from 'Those who owned the machine . . .' to the end of the passage for your answer.)
7 Explain the metaphor of those 'who came to reap and harvest where they had not ploughed or planted.'

8 What are the meanings of the following phrases:
  - The true lesson of history
  - oppression and exploitation
  - the inherited inventive genius of man
  - all ages and climes
  - monopoly of a few

Further discussion

1 A *Utopia* has been defined as 'an ideally perfect place or state of things.'

  a Do you think Ngugi's 'human kingdom' can be described as a Utopia rather than as a realistic view of the future?

  b Some people say that descriptions of Utopias are good as they give us hope in the future. Others say they are bad as they distort reality. What do *you* think?

2 The first passage in this chapter sees history as repetitive and unchanging, not least of all because of the unchanging character of human nature. The second passage suggests that only a small elite of specially talented people can possibly bring about change. The last two passages are more hopeful about the future and feel that change rests with the working people.

  a Do you agree that the passages can be grouped in this way? Why?

  b With which view would you agree and why?

3 The last two passages are quite different in their content and style while trying to put across a similar viewpoint.

  a Discuss the similarities and differences between these two passages.

  b Which did you prefer? Why?

Creative writing

Write a composition entitled simply **The Future**. You could write a story or another character sketch, or a discussion of your views.

Book list

KOFI AWOONOR   *This Earth, My Brother* . . ., Heinemann, 1971, pp. 30 & 92.

WOLE SOYINKA   *Season of Anomy*, Rex Collings, 1973, pp. 136, 174 & 176.

SEMBENE OUSMANE   'Chaiba the Algerian', in *Tribal Scars*, Heinemann, 1974, pp. 81 – 3.

NGUGI WA THIONG'O   *Petals of Blood*, Heinemann, 1977, pp. 303 & 304.

Section B: Themes

Men and wheelbarrow H. Budaza

Work

Many writers have dealt with the subject of work. This is because it is so absolutely important to people – without earning a living people cannot afford food, shelter, education for their children etc. There are two passages in the following chapter that show how terrible unemployment is.

Even those with work, however, are often forced by their employers to work very hard for very low wages, as many of the other passages in this section show.

Work takes up much of a person's lifetime. It is, therefore, a big problem when the work is boring, the conditions in which the person works are bad and the rewards for labour are small.

Think about the work that you would like to do and also about what you can and should expect from it.

Servants – 1

Diouana, a young Senegalese girl has been brought to France by the French family she worked for while the latter were living in Africa.

The days and weeks had gone by and Diouana was starting on her third month. She was no longer a lively, laughing young woman. Her eyes were sunken and dulled, and her glance failed to take things in. She had far more work to do than ever she had in Africa. She was eating her heart out, and her old friends would hardly have recognised her. France, beautiful France was but a vague image, a fleeting vision; all she knew of it was the unkempt garden, the evergreen hedges of the other villas, and their roofs poking up above the green trees and palm-trees. Everyone seemed to live his own life, shut away in his house. Her master and mistress often went out, leaving her with the four children. They had soon ganged up against her and were always plaguing her. . . .

Everything became blurred, dissolved and vanished – the life she had dreamed about, the happiness she had thought to have. She was worked off her feet. She was cook, nursemaid and laundress all in one. Madame's sister had come to stay at the villa, so there were seven people to look after. When she was at last able to go up to bed, she fell asleep at once and slept like a log.

Venom entered her heart; she had never had any reason to hate people before. Everything became monotonous and dreary. She wondered where France was – the France of the fine cities she had seen on the screen in Dakar cinemas, of delicious food and dense crowds? The people of France were reduced to these unkind brats and to Monsieur, Madame and Mademoiselle, who had become strangers to her. The whole country contracted to the boundaries of the villa. Slowly but surely, she was sinking under it all. . . .

Bewildered by her small knowledge of French, Diouana withdrew into herself even more. She ruminated over her situation and came to the conclusion that she was nothing but a useful object and that her employers showed her off as if she were some trophy or other. When they had guests in for the evening they sometimes talked about the psychology of the 'natives', and took her as an example. The neighbours called her 'their black servant'. But she was not black to herself, and that wounded her.

As time passed, everything got worse and she saw more clearly. She had more work than she could cope with, from one week's end to the next. The Lord's Day was Mademoiselle's favourite time for inviting her friends, and the house became filled with them. One week ended with them, and the next began with them.

It was all quite plain to her now. Why had Madame been so anxious for her to come? There had been calculation behind the gifts and the little extras. Madame no longer looked after the children; she kissed them when they got up in the morning, and that was all. And what had happened to that beautiful France? Diouana had seen nothing of it. These questions kept going through her mind. I'm cook, nursemaid and chambermaid, I do all the washing and iron it, and all for a pittance, three thousand francs a month. I do the work of six people. So why am I here?

SEMBENE OUSMANE   'The Promised Land', from *Tribal Scars*

Questions

1 a Describe in detail the work Diouana had to do.

  b In what ways were things even more difficult for her than they would have been for a French maid working for the same family?

2 a What kind of picture of life in France did some Africans in Dakar have?

  b Do you think that Diouana had been happy and eager to come to France with her employers? Quote from the passage to back up your answer.

3 What did Madame do to persuade her to come with them to France?

4 Describe in your own words why Diouana's old friends would hardly have recognised her.

5 How do we know that Diouana gets paid very little for all her hard work?

6 Explain the following:

  a 'The whole country contracted to the boundaries of the villa.'

  b '. . . her employers showed her off as if she were some trophy or other.'

  c 'The neighbours called her 'their black servant'. But she was not black to herself, and that wounded her.'

  d 'There had been calculation behind the gifts and the little extras.'

7 Make sentences with the following:
- unkempt
- plaguing
- monotonous
- bewildered
- ruminated

Servants – 2

Timi and Karabo have emigrated from South Africa and have come to an independent African country:

After two years Timi and Karabo resigned themselves to the situation. They had tried to ward it off – the necessity, if not the need, of keeping a servant. The first month of his arrival in Sogali, Timi had cleaned his own house and cooked his own breakfast. He then decided to cook his own dinner: it was proving too expensive to eat in a restaurant – . . .

'Got a good steward?' one of Timi's colleagues asked him.

'No, I don't want one.'

'Why not? you can't do all that housework alone, you know!'

Frequently he was harassed by the same question, until he suspected that he was being considered abnormal or a snob.

'Excuse me, sah,' a student said to him one afternoon.

'Yes, Ilorin?'

'I live with my second mother and she has many other children so there's no room and I-I'm asking the master if I can come and live in your steward's quarters and clean and cook for you.' . . .

Timi found it necessary to rationalise himself out of the situation. Ilorin was a student, and he needed help. He took him on.

Several men had come to the house to ask for work as a steward. He simply could not imagine a person working for him: washing, cleaning, handling his bodily dirt, waiting on him at table. How could he, whose mother had been a domestic servant for whites for all those years, take over the white man's role as master? How could he look himself in the mirror after degrading himself like that? He could never think of a master-servant relationship as a normal one that could be tidy, clean. So he had told the applicants politely that he did not need a servant. His colleagues had even said outright that by refusing the services of a steward he was doing at least one man out of a livelihood. The more Timi debated the thing in his mind, the more confused, the more exasperating the issue became. But he took Ilorin and told himself *So far, no further!* . . .

Karabo arrived, after Ilorin had been with him for five months. She was no less outraged by the idea of a servant. 'What! a black man have servants?' she said. She decided to keep Ilorin. He was good protection. But the men continued to come. 'Let your wife come,' Efu, Awoonor's wife had said. 'Let her decide what to do. But she's not goin' to find it easy without a steward. I'm born here, but I still find I need at least two – steward to help cook, clean the house, do the washin', and a helper – just a small boy – to wash the dishes, help with the floors. The heat will be worse on your wife.'

Timi had waited for Karabo's reaction.

She had tried it for a month, then said one day, 'No, Timi, Efu was right. This heat wears me out and the children's clothes just keep piling up.'

'Will you feel happy if we employ a steward and Ilorin can then be more of a helper?'

'I don't want to do it, Timi, the idea disgusts me and I could cry just to think of someone else's man kneeling on the floors to do the work I should be doing. I simply won't know how to instruct him what to do. But I'll do my own cooking.'

'Maybe Doris or Florence or Frances can advise us. . . .'

'Huh, black-white suburbia talking about servant problems, eh!'

'That's right. That's the order of the day.'

The words tasted like heartburn in his mouth.

And so Karabo and Timi were instructed on servants. . . .

Try as he might, Timi failed to talk like the traditional master. Always he thought of the white master and the black servant in South Africa. Why did he have to take a seat in the row of masters? He gave up trying to speak like one.

EZEKIEL MPHAHLELE   *The Wanderers*

Questions

1 a Why did Timi eventually employ Ilorin?

   b What does it mean to 'rationalise himself out of the situation'?

2 There were *two* kinds of pressure working on Timi and Karabo to make them employ a servant – pressure from outsiders and pressure from within their own domestic situation. Give examples of both of these kinds of pressure. Which do you think in the end was more important? Why?

3 Describe in detail and in your own words why both Timi and Karabo felt so great an unwillingness to employ servants.

4 a How do we know that Timi and Karabo had always felt that it was only *whites* who employed servants?

   b What is the meaning of 'black-white suburbia'? How does this concept cut across seeing the situation purely in terms of race (Blacks and Whites)?

5 From what was Ilorin supposed to be 'good protection'?

6 Why do you think Karabo insists that she will do her own cooking?

7 In what way did Timi not succeed as a 'traditional master'?

8 Can you think of an answer to Timi's rhetorical question: 'Why did he have to take a seat in the row of masters?'?

9 a Find one word in the passage meaning each of the following:
     • somebody who works in the same job as someone
     • very troubled and worried by something
     • a person who thinks that he/she is better than everybody else
     • frustrating

   b Now make sentences with each of these words.

10 Re-write in your own words:
     • resigned themselves to the situation
     • ward it off
     • degrading himself
     • He could never think of a master-servant relationship as a normal one that could be tidy, clean.
     • The words tasted like heartburn in his mouth.

Further discussion

The whole question of servants – their hours, pay, living quarters etc., sometimes even whether one should employ servants in the home at all – is quite a heated one. What do *you* think concerning these issues?

Creative writing

1 Make up your own employer and servant situation.
   or
2 Describe in detail one day in Diouana's life.
   or
3 Describe an incident in Timi and Karabo's house centering around a servant whom they eventually employ.

Nel comes to town

Nel has come to Port Elizabeth looking for work. She finds a job in a second-hand clothing shop:

That first day in Port Elizabeth Nel told Mr Levy only about the family in Prince Albert and her reason for leaving them.

'We saved up, my brother Bokkie and me,' she said, 'for trainfare. Bokkie first went to Graaff-Reinet to see about Maria, that's my sister, for our mother, but I came here. I thought it's a big city. I thought it's the best place to come look for work to send money home.'

Mr Levy sympathised. He knew what poverty was. He would help her. But then (and one must be honest) he knew also that girls like Nel who came from farms and small towns made good, hard workers. He had had such simple, unspoilt girls working for him before. Of course it was only a matter of time before they 'went to pot', before the bioscopes, dancing and boyfriends meant more to them than their jobs. Until then, though, they worked as hard as blacks, and for almost as little.

'Okay,' Mr Levy said. 'Start tomorrow half past seven. We open at eight, but we dust, pack the stock, tidy first. . . .' Nel worked hard at the shop and within a very short time proved herself to be a remarkably able assistant. She had of course had a long and intimate association with second-hand clothing. She could tell, from the mere feel of a garment, from the state of its seams, the weave of the cloth, how long it would last, the sort of person to whom it was most likely to appeal and what it was worth.

Unlike some of the other assistants Mr Levy had had, Nel was not patronising towards the Whites who came to buy; as for the non-Whites who made up the greater part of his clientele, there was no difference at all in Nel's treatment of them. She did not say 'Yes?' and 'What do you want?' as though they were wasting her time. Nor did she ever say 'Come on, come on, I haven't got all day!'

She was the best assistant Mr Levy had ever had and after a while he allowed her, at the end of every month, the pick of the stock, and at cost price too, so that her own living expenses remained low enough to enable her to send a few pounds home to Naomi, as well as the clothes which Naomi could alter to fit the children.

Nel could not handle every situation, but whenever she was at a loss Mr Levy would come forward to help, as he did once when a White woman, heavily made up and wearing a thin cotton frock although it was cold outside, came in to stand dancing to music which only she could hear. She took no notice of Nel's polite offer to serve her, and when Mr Levy saw that Nel was incapable of being firm, he took the woman's arm and as he led her out, Nel saw that her ankle was quite purple and swollen to twice its normal size. It could not have been as painful as it looked, considering the way she had been jiggling about on it, but, as Mr Levy explained afterwards, she had been blind drunk and when in that state, 'they can't feel a thing, not even pain, you know . . .'.

Apart from such incidents, Nel liked her job. She could not reasonably ask for anything more from life, she told herself, if only she could find a better place to live.

YVONNE BURGESS   A Life to Live

Questions

1 Why did Nel want a job in Port Elizabeth?
2 Give two reasons why Mr Levy employed Nel. Which do you think was more important? Why?
3 How do we know that Mr Levy paid Nel very little?
4 Why had Nel *of course* had 'a long and intimate association with second-hand clothing.'?
5 a What is the meaning of *patronising*?
   b Why do you think some of the other assistants had been patronising towards White customers?
6 How do we know that Nel was not a racist?
7 How did Mr Levy reward Nel for being so efficient?
8 How do we know that Nel
   a spent very little money on herself;
   b had dreadful living conditions in Port Elizabeth and
   c was too accepting of the poor quality of her life?
9 Describe the incident of the drunken White woman.

10 How do we know that she too was very poor?

11 Find one word in the passage for:
- article of clothing
- customers
- goods for sale in the shop
- a dress
- dancing

Town Life: Journalism in Johannesburg in the 1950's

Someone had passed the buck to me. The story went out that a razor-sharp journalist from Durban was coming to Johannesburg to work in our main office. The editor had told someone to find accommodation for him, and that someone had decided that his initiation was best in my hands. In those days handing an other-town boy into my hands for initiation was subtlest excruciation. Not that we would persecute him, we only sought to divest him of the naïvetés and extraneous moralities with which we knew he would be encumbered.

He came, I remember, in the morning with a suitcase and a tennis racket – ye hods, a tennis racket! We stared at him. The chaps on *Drum* at that time had fancied themselves to be poised on a dramatic, implacable kind of life. Journalism was still new to most of us and we saw it in the light of the heroics of Henry Nxumalo, decidedly not in the light of tennis, which we classed with draughts.

He had a puckish, boyish face, and a name something like Nathaniel Nakasa. We soon made it Nat. I took him to Sophiatown and showed him the room where he would stay – what was it? Three minutes, five minutes? Then I took him to my *shebeen* in Edith Street. . . .

Honest, I don't know how it happened, but I left him there. He told me later, that a few *tsotsis* came in and he approached them with trepidated terror. He asked them if they knew where Can Themba lived and they immediately looked hostile. (At first, they thought he contemplated some harm to the revered Can Themba.) But when Mpho, the girl, explained that this was really a friend of the chap, who had deserted him there in one of his drunken impulses, they said, 'O.K. Durbanboy, hang around and we'll take you there.'

This is a measure of Nat's character. He was in a new situation. He knew about Jo'burg tsotsis, the country's worst. He was scared – he told me later he was. But he went with them, chatted with them, wanted to know what type of character this, his host, was. Though he got only grunts, it was the journalist in action, not the terrified fish out of water.

He found me at home, out of this world's concerns. Later, he found out about Jo'burg without the aid of my derelictions. He quickly learned about the united nations of Fordsburg and Malay Camp; about the liberal enclaves in Hillbrow; about the cosmopolitanism of Johannesburg.

CAN THEMBA   The Will to Die

Questions

1 a How do we know from the first sentence of the passage that the narrator is unwilling to look after the new journalist from Durban?

   b What incident later on in the passage confirms this?

2 a How do we know from the second sentence in the passage that the new journalist was experienced in the job?

   b Describe in detail an incident later on in the passage that proves this.

3 a Find a word in the first paragraph that means each of the following:
  - act against somebody, harass or worry them
  - points of ethics, system of behaviour
  - hampered or burdened
  - inappropriate, not belonging to something
  - terrible torture
  - introduction of a new person into something (like a job)
  - artlessness, amusing simplicity
  - strip someone of something

   b Now re-write the two sentences beginning 'In those days'. . . and ending with 'which we knew he would be encumbered', in your own words.

   c Do you think that all the long words in these two sentences are effective (add anything to the passage)? Why?

4 Why were the other journalists shocked by the newcomer's tennis racket?

5 Work out from the passage the meaning of

   a shebeen

   b tsotsi

6 What is a 'fish out of water'?

7 a Why do you think that Fordsburg is described as the 'united nations'?

   b What are 'liberal enclaves'?

   c What is cosmopolitanism?

Further discussion

Can Themba and Nat Nakasa are urban Black South Africans and Nel is a rural White South African.

a What is the definition of *a stereotype*? (Remember you can use your dictionary to help you).

b In what way is the description of these journalists and of Nel a breakdown of stereotype? (Think of all the stories that have been written about Blacks coming into the big city and the Whites they meet there.)

Creative writing

1 Describe a day in the life of *either* a journalist on Drum magazine *or* of Nel in the second-hand clothing shop.

or

2 Write a description of a sleepy little village *or* of a big city that you know.

Unemployment – 1

Zeca is desperately searching for work. His friend, Maneco, speaks to him about it. The story is set in Angola still during Portuguese occupation.

Maneco turned the conversation.

'Ya got anything yet?'

'Nothing, Maneco.' . . . More than a week now I'm looking for work and there's nothing!'

Maneco lit another cigarette then spat into the water, 'And that one from the newspaper. Did ya go?'

'Not yet.'

'Better go and try today, ya never know . . .'

'Oh they're not going to take me. I'm too thin and they say "office and warehouse" in that newspaper. You know already it means heavy work.'

Maneco opened the clipping and read the ad aloud, slowly looking at each letter – he didn't have much schooling and reading fast was hard for him. When he finished he leapt to his feet like a cat and playfully slapped Zeca on the back, 'Let's go, kid!'

Maneco was always calling him kid when he was going to help Zeca with something; knowing this by now, Zeca smiled. At his friend's side, feeling his head begin to spin and the brilliant sea tremble, he said, 'I'll go myself, Maneco. . . .'

Twilight was coming and the sun burned its way towards the sea, leaving not one cloud in the blue sky and attacking the Downtown, defenceless without trees. Zeca Santos' stomach was not complaining now but the heat was all over his body, making his feet itch so that he walked fast through all the people, his yellow shirt turning this way and that as he tried not to bump into them. He approached the place of the ad with courage, already arranging in his head the words, the reasons – he would talk about his old grandma, it didn't matter what the work was they might want to give him, he would take it . . .

. . . A tall thin man stood in front of him, looking at the notice in his hand. Zeca was about to speak but the man just shoved him to the errand boy's table.

'Yes, I know, I know. Don't say anything! You've come about the ad, right? Over here. Xico, oh Xico!'

The boy in the uniform came running with a notebook and pencil, then stopped in front of him, expectantly. The thin man looked carefully into Zeca Santos' eyes and suddenly burst out with a lot of questions like he wanted to make Zeca nervous: where did he work? what did he do? how much did he earn? if he was married who was the family? was he an *assimilado?* did he have a letter of good behaviour from other bosses? and lots of other things giving Zeca Santos no time to answer at all. Finally, when Zeca was trembling from the cold office air and the emptiness eating at his belly and voices fading farther and farther away the man loomed up before him eyeing his shirt and his tight trousers with suspicion and distrust.

'Listen here, boy, where were you born?'

'Where you born?' repeated the errand boy.

'Catete, boss.'

The man whistled and taking his glasses away from his tired eyes, he struck the table, 'From Catete, huh? *Icolibengo?** Uppity, lazy good-for-nothing thieves! And what's more, terrorists now! Get out of here . . . I don't want Catetes in here!'

JOSÉ LUANDINO VIEIRA   Luanda

Questions

1 What are all the reasons that Zeca does not stand much of a chance of getting a job?
2 How do we know that Maneco is a very good friend of Zeca's and has helped him many times before?
3 Why was Zeca's head spinning?
4 What do you imagine Zeca would say about his grandmother?

---

*Icolibengo Portuguese: a geographical region north of Luanda known to the Portuguese authorities as a centre of strong nationalist sentiments and activities (specifically of the Movement for the Liberation of Angola, MPLA). It was the birthplace of Dr. Antonio Agostinho Neto, leader of the MPLA during the war of liberation and Angola's first President after independence.

5 Why did the tall, thin man ask Zeca so many questions if he did not allow him to reply to them?

6 What does the word 'shoved' tell us about the man's attitude to Zeca?

7 What does the word 'loomed' tell us about Zeca's attitude to the man?

8 Describe in detail why Zeca does not, in the end, get the job. (Look at the note below the passage). Do you think that that is fair? Why?

9 Do you imagine that he would have got the job anyway? Why?

10 Re-write in indirect speech from the beginning of the passage to '"... you know already it means heavy work"'.

11 Writers often use descriptions of the weather or scenery to help us understand their characters' emotions, lives and so on. Find *two* examples in the passage where Vieira does this in order to help him to describe Zeca's problems.

12 Make sentences with the following:
  • defenceless
  • courage
  • expectantly
  • suspicion
  • distrust

Unemployment – 2

Meja searches for work in Nairobi. His friend, Maina, has long given up hope of finding a job:

He walked for the whole day from office to office until his feet were tired and sore. He talked to anybody he thought might be able to help, from office boys to managers. Few wanted even to hear him sing out his qualifications or to know whether he had any. But undaunted he carried on. He repeated his piece in so many offices that he became addicted to it. He said it without thinking and this did not make matters any better. Late in the afternoon he went into a big office and found the manager and the secretary.

The manager, obviously sleepy from the effects of a heavy lunch, looked up lazily from his work. Meja looking his most humble, stood at the door and the two stared at one another for a moment. The manager was trying to focus his thoughts on the newcomer and the other waited for permission to speak. Then the manager woke up.

'Well, what do you want?' he asked.

Meja breathed hard and put on his most intelligent look in an effort to cover his misery.

'First division School Certificate,' he announced.

The manager took his cigar from the corner of his lips, placed it on the ash tray, took off his spectacles next and then scrutinized Meja. He took the youth in slowly and deliberately, the way a scientist studies a specimen. . . .

Then: 'Well, what about it?' the manager spoke to the young man.

Meja's heart faltered then recovered and hammered in his chest. He licked his lips.

'I . . . I want a job . . . vacancy,' he said.

The manager put his glasses back on, apparently satisfied that his adversary was harmless and stuck his cigar back at the corner of his lips. He chewed at it, sucked strongly and emitted a thick black cloud.

'How did you come in here?' he asked.

'I . . . I came,' Meja could not possibly guess what was expected of him.

'Through the main door, I presume,' the big man said.

Meja nodded and said a dry 'yes'.

'Can you read?' the man asked.

Hope soared through Meja. His voice trembled with ecstasy.

'Yes . . . yes,' he said, 'I can also write.'

'Then you ought to have written down your request,' the other said. 'Anyhow . . .'

He pressed a blue button on his desk . . . A messenger walked into the office and stood at attention.

'Go with him,' the manager said to Meja and went back to scanning some forms that needed signing.

Meja's thoughts were unfathomable as he followed the messenger down the many winding stairs. His mind raced ahead of him. A job at last. The two reached the ground floor and the huge glass doors. The messenger led him to the big doors and showed him the tiny white letters painted on one of the doors.

It took Meja one long minute to grasp the meaning of it all. And then he understood and could not believe. He could not believe that the messenger had gone to all that trouble to show him this. Yet the letters were there staring boldly back at him. They screamed in two tongues: NO VACANCY. HAKUNA KAZI . . .

Meja never went into offices again to look for work. He followed Maina's example and tried to forget that he ever went to school and wanted a job. The thought of his family back home haunted him for a few weeks though – of his parents expecting to hear the good news that he had a job, not knowing that that was exactly the bit of news that they were least likely ever to hear. Yet even had he the courage to go back and tell them the truth, there was the problem of bus fare. So he tucked the memories of his family into the darkest corner of his mind, put on a resigned smile and followed his friend faithfully wherever he went.

Maina taught him a lot of things. He taught him how to look after himself and how to avoid getting involved in other people's business, least of all policemen's. When a policeman was on the beat he did not like to be interfered with, not even if that beat happened to trespass on your sleeping bin. The boys fetched food from bins, slept in bins and lived in the backyards, in bins.

MEJA MWANGI *Kill Me Quick*

Questions

1 a Write out the sentence in the passage that tells us that schooling did not help boys like Meja to find jobs.
  b Why do you think that this was the case?
2 a Why do you think the writer tells us about the manager having just eaten a heavy lunch?
  b What is the effect of the following description of the manager:
    '. . . (he) stuck his cigar back at the corner of his lips. He chewed at it, sucked strongly and emitted a thick black cloud.'
3 a How does the manager turn down Meja's request for a job?
  b Do you think that the way he did it was cruel? Why?
4 For what *two* reasons did Meja not contact his family?
5 In your own words describe what Maina taught Meja, and how the boys lived.
6 a Some metaphors (comparisons) are used so often in a certain way that one forgets that comparisons are being used at all. Study the following examples and, in each case, describe what is being compared:
    • 'The manager was trying to focus his thoughts on the newcomer'
    • 'Meja's heart . . . hammered in his chest.'
    • 'His mind raced ahead of him.'
    • 'So he tucked the memories of his family into the darkest corner of his mind'
  b Do you think that these metaphors are very effective? Why?
7 Explain what is being compared in the following simile:
  'He took the youth in slowly and deliberately, the way a scientist studies a specimen.'
8 Find *one* word in the passage for each of the following:
  • refusing to be discouraged or put off
  • examine very closely
  • great happiness and joy
  • unable to be understood or described.

Further discussion

1 Compare and contrast Zeca and Meja. What do you imagine are the deep effects of continued unemployment on people?
2 Compare the 'tall thin man' of the previous passage with the manager in the passage above. Can you try to account for the similarities between them?

Creative writing

Make up a character of your own who is unemployed, and describe his/her desperate search for work.

Workers – 1

In 1947 – 8 the railway workers on the Dakar – Niger line came out on strike:

When they had finished eating, the men began to gather in front of the gate, and soon there was a tangle of bicycles and motor scooters leaning against the fence that surrounded the yards. On a normal day they would have gone quickly to their respective shops, but today they just hung about at the entrance. They were all there – the men who worked on the trains themselves and the laborers from the marshaling yards, the switchmen and the office workers – those who should have been on duty and those who were not.

The great gate was open, but in the main court there was just one man. Leaning heavily on his cane, Sounkaré, the head watchman, surveyed the crowd with an expression of astonishment on his face and then made his way, in his awkward, crab-like gait, toward a group of the old men who were standing by themselves.

'This is strange,' he said, after greeting them.

'Very strange, indeed,' Bakary replied, between two fits of coughing. 'But soon we will know what is going to happen.'

Bakary was tuberculous, and no one who saw him could have failed to know it. The years behind the firebox of the trains had turned the skin of his face to gray and covered it with tough film, like callus.

'So they are not going to work?' the watchman muttered. 'They have short memories, these children! But you. . . .' he turned to the group of old men. 'Surely you will not follow them?'

'That's just what we were talking about. Some of them came to see us this morning, to ask if we agreed with their demands.'

'What demands?' asked Sounkaré, 'I have demanded nothing.' He paused and laughed. 'But then, I don't have much longer to live.'

'You are not as ill as I am, Sounkaré,' Bakary said. 'The sickness in my chest will be with me always. I thought they were talking just about salaries, but I went to their meetings, and I found that they were talking about a pension, too – a pension that would affect us, and not just the young ones. Look around you . . .' he coughed and turned his head to spit a little ball of black phlegm into the dust. 'Look around you. There are not very many of us any more. Where are all the others – Aliou Samba, and Abdoulaye, and Coulibaly, and the Davids who came from the island of

91

Gorée – they had no pension, and now they are dead. Soon it will be our turn, and what are we to live on? And the fathers of the white men, the ones who taught us our trade – the Edouards and the Henris and the Delacollines – where are they? They are living at home again, and they have their pensions. Why should we not have this pension, too? That is what the young ones are asking.'

'Ha! I can see that these children have led you astray. God in His wisdom may help you, Bakary, but the *toubabs* may refuse. From here to Koulikoro, everything that moves belongs to them. Even our lives belong to them.'

'Don't mix religion in this. Perhaps it is true that it is the will of God, but we must live. And is it not written, "God loves to help him who strives to help himself"!' . . .

The first blast of the siren seemed longer than usual. The silence gripped them again; a silence which rendered movement, and even thought, impossible.

The great entrance gate still stood open, but no one moved toward it. When the siren screamed again, a shudder went through the crowd. The sound seemed to enter into their bodies, to mingle with their blood. For as long as they could remember, that sound had meant obedience. As children they had seen their fathers, and even their grandfathers, begin to run when they heard it call. It had always told them when to leave their houses, and to walk up here and pass through the gate, and it had punctuated their working day. . . .

It was Samba N'Doulougou – a difficult name to remember, but more difficult still to forget – who was the first to recover. Jumping up into Boubacar's shoulders, he cried out, 'Hurrah for the strike!' – and then, perched on his friend's back, he began shouting to the crowd in Bambara.

That was when the soldiers charged.

SEMBENE OUSMANE *God's Bits of Wood*

Questions

1 What sort of workers were assembled in front of the gate?
2 Why did some of the old men support the strike?
3 What was wrong with Bakary and what had caused his illness?
4 a Why did Sounkaré not support the strike?
   b Writers sometimes describe what their characters look like in order to help explain what kind of people they are. How does the description of the way Sounkaré walks help to do this?
5 Describe in detail and in your own words why the sound of the siren had such a big effect on the people.
6 What finally made the soldiers charge against the workers?

7 Re-write in your own words:
- 'soon there was a tangle of bicycles and motor scooters'
- 'these children have led you astray.'
- 'a silence which rendered movement, and even thought, impossible.'
- '(the siren) had punctuated their working day.'
- 'perched on his friend's back'

8 Make sentences with the following:
- astonishment
- awkward
- strives
- shudder
- obedience

Workers – 2

Idemudia has started a new job on a building site:

A gong sounded and startled him out of his thoughts. He did not stand up immediately but looked around at the other workers. He saw them all, one after the other, dusting the seat of their shorts or trousers. He saw them standing up. The break was over. He stood up from the heap of gravel and went towards the mixer. Patrick and Omoifo were already gone.

Osaro confronted him at once. 'What are you thinking about?' he demanded.

'It is bad,' he answered. 'The pay, the work, the site, everything.'

'You are not forced to stay on,' Osaro chided him.

'How can you say that?' Idemudia asked. 'Why do you say I am not forced to stay on? If I went away, how would I eat? How would I pay my rent? How would I survive? I stay because I have nowhere better to go.'

Osaro dropped the stone he was holding in his hands. 'I was only joking,' he admitted. 'I have never been in a place like this before. The labourers do not talk, they whisper. They are afraid. Remember that other place where we had that strike? It wasn't half as bad as here.'

They fell silent as they fed the concrete mixer. The men came again and again and each time they brought the wheelbarrows, and headpans and the buckets. Their chests glistened with sweat, their backs were bathed in sweat. They worked in subdued silence like prisoners, coming and going in the intense light of the sun. . . .

The sun continued to bear down mercilessly. And one after another, the men removed their shirts until their backs glistened with the sweat from labouring. The mixer turned round slowly, insatiable as the men fed the gravel, the cement and the other materials. The wheelbarrow drivers came

93

and went, then came back for more and not far off, the vibrator worked noisily as the men tried to keep the cement from sinking to the bottom in the several pits.

Where the houses were struggling up was like a scene of battle. The land was upturned, hoisted and flung in several directions. The bush was held back by the piles of gravel and sand but here and there some green grasses had taken root and now boasted flowers with yellow petals, small tongues of yellow fever which dangled, danced, shivered and sliced through the wind.

FESTUS IYAYI   *Violence*

Questions

1 Describe in detail, and in your own words what work the men are doing on the building site, and under what conditions.

2 a Explain why Idemudia disagrees with Osaro when he says that Idemudia could leave the job if he wanted to.

   b What is being compared in the following simile?
   'They worked in subdued silence like prisoners . . .'

   c Is it a good (apt) comparison? Why?

   d Pick out another simile in the passage and state what is being compared and whether the comparison is apt (appropriate, good).

3 a What is the writer trying to emphasize in his repetition of the word 'glistened' in the passage?

   b Why are the yellow flowers compared to 'small tongues of yellow fever'?

   c Describe the movement of the flowers in the wind. Why are they described in that way?

4 How does the description of the burning sun add to the atmosphere in the passage?

5 Make sentences with the following words:
   - startled
   - confronted
   - chided
   - subdued
   - insatiable

Further discussion

1 Discuss what you imagine happens after the soldiers have charged in the previous passage.

2 There is a great deal of *tension* (strained feelings, anger etc.) in the last passage. Discuss what you imagine happens on the building site as conditions worsen.

3 What is a strike? Do you think it is an effective way for workers to address their grievances? Why?

94

Creative writing

We have looked at a few different kinds of jobs and also at the horror of unemployment. Write an essay entitled *Work* and discuss some of the issues raised in this chapter and/or any other issues you feel are important on this topic.

What job would *you* like to have? Describe it in some detail and give reasons for your choice.

Book list

EZEKIEL MPHAHLELE   *The Wanderers,* Fontana, 1973, pp. 178 – 181.

SEMBENE OUSMANE   'The Promised Land', in *Tribal Scars*, Heinemann, 1974, pp. 94 – 5 & 97.

CAN THEMBA   *The Will to Die*, Heinemann, 1972, pp. 99 – 100.

YVONNE BURGESS   *A Life to Live,* A.D. Donker, 1973, pp. 47 & 58 – 9.

JOSÉ LUANDINO VIEIRA   *Luanda*, Heinemann, 1980, pp. 16 – 18.

MEJA MWANGI   *Kill Me Quick*, Heinemann, 1973, pp. 4 – 5 & 9.

SEMBENE OUSMANE   *God's Bits of Wood,* Heinemann, 1970, pp. 17 – 18, 21 & 22.

FESTUS IYAYI   *Violence*, Longman, 1979, pp. 251 – 2 & 255.

The Workers H. Budaza

Women and Marriage

We have seen in previous chapters that writers are very concerned with the changes that have taken place on their continent in the last few decades. These have included social, political and economic changes as well as changes in values, customs and life-styles. We will notice the same kind of concern in the following passages.

These passages all concentrate on women – the division of labour between men and women, social attitudes to women and the institution of marriage. The writers (both men and women) have different views on women and marriage while they all seek to explain the position of women in the social order which they describe.

Many writers, both male and female, are opposed to the custom of polygamy (a man taking more than one wife), and also to the passing of money from the man's to the woman's family when a marriage is sealed. There is also a great deal of thought about the modern status (standing) of women in the home and in the society – things have both changed and remained the same in the way men regard women, and women regard themselves.

Read the passages carefully, answer the questions, and decide for yourselves what you feel about these issues.

Marriage and Money

Essola has come out from ten years in detention to find that his young sister, Perpetua, has been married and has died. He has this argument with his mother. (She is talking):

'Every woman is meant for marriage, it's the law of nature, and that's that. I swear when I married Perpetua I only thought about her happiness and the Law of God. I found a husband for my daughter and she received him favourably because he suited her and they liked each other. . . .'

He had allowed her to go on. Suddenly Essola struck back with almost murderous fury.

'Do you know,' he told her, 'ever since I found out that Perpetua had been married and had died, not a single night has passed that I have not dwelt in my sleeplessness on this unhappy business, going over it again and again, taking it all to pieces. And, mother, I have always come to the same simple reason for this dreadful tragedy. When I was sentenced and detained, when I was in trouble, mother, you were glad. That wasn't right, it wasn't, mother . . . You were glad because you thought now you would have a free hand. I had given my word that Perpetua would never marry any man unless she wanted to. You knew that very well, mother. I had given my word that no one would put pressure on Perpetua. You knew that, didn't you mother? And, especially, I had given my word that Perpetua would not be sold, that no one would touch a penny on her head, that she would be a free wife. You knew that, didn't you, mother? Well, after I was detained you thought you could get a wife for your son, Martin, who is the most useless man in the world, because he is the king of idleness. So you thought the time had come to sell my little Perpetua. And in the end, you sold her and laid your plans in favour of your favourite son. And that was the crime that had to lead to this tragedy. Well, I tell you this, mother. Because you sold Perpetua, the murderer of Perpetua is you. . . .'

Later Essola's cousin talks to him:

'. . . In spite of all you've been through you haven't really changed. You still believe that the blackman can follow the rules of life of the *Toubab*, the whiteman.'

'It's nothing to do with the rules of life, *Frérot*. It's to do with Perpetua, my sister, your cousin. I didn't want her to be sold, I didn't want her to become some man's slave.'

'Don't talk so loud, I'm not deaf. Slave, it's an easy word to say. Money changed hands when our mothers were married. Did that make them slaves?'

'Yes, of course, it did.'

'It's not surprising you never have any peace of mind, *Frérot*. With ideas like that, you will go raving mad, unless you kill someone first, or someone kills you. . . .'

Towards the end of the novel, the writer thinks about Perpetua's early death:

So Perpetua departed at twenty, leaving the supposed banquet of life at the age, when elsewhere, others are just being allowed to take their places for the first time in all the splendour of their glittering youth, like the bright train of some exquisite bride.

Was it not better, when all things were considered, that it should be so? To die with her first charm all about her, provided with all her teeth, without a wrinkle. To die, not worn out and shrivelled, withered and faded, but strong, sturdy and supple, fresh and firm, as if falling asleep in the evening before making love – was this really an outrage crying to the ears of a brother for vengeance?

What would have become of Perpetua? To find out, he only needed to look around in Zombotown, that graveyard of the female living dead, swarming with ghosts that spoke eloquently of Perpetua. Battered, broken by life, demeaned, deadened; by thirty, swollen up with water and useless fat . . .

MONGO BETI   *Perpetua and the Habit of Unhappiness*

Questions

1 What are Perpetua's mother's views on women and marriage? Do you agree with her? Why?

2 In what way did Essola stand in the way of his mother's plans?

3 What do you think a 'free wife' is?

4 a Who was the mother's favourite son?
   b Why was her mother so keen to arrange a marriage for Perpetua?

5 Describe in your own words the disagreement between Essola and his cousin. Who do you think is right? Why?

6 The writer is not *really* suggesting that it was good for Perpetua to die young. He only seems to be saying so in order to stress his main point about the women in Zombotown (and elsewhere). In your own words describe the point he is making.

7 A *paradox* is a statement that seems impossible and contradictory, but looked at closely holds a lot of truth. In what way is the description of 'the female living dead' a paradox?

8 Find *one* word in the passage for each of the following:
   - insomnia
   - extremely beautiful
   - revenge
   - humiliated – made to seem as nothing

9 Make a sentence with each of the following:
   - favourably
   - shrivelled
   - supple

10 Re-write in indirect speech from '"In spite of all . . ."' to '". . . kills you."'

11 a Explain what is being compared in the following metaphor: 'banquet of life'.

  b What is being compared in the following simile: 'in all the splendour of their glittering youth, like the bright train of some exquisite bride'.

  c Do the metaphor 'banquet of life' and this simile come together well? (i.e. Do they help each other?) Explain.

Her Three Days

Noumbe is one of Mustapha's wives. Mustapha, according to polygamous custom, is supposed to spend three days with each wife in turn. It is now Noumbe's turn to have 'her three days':

She knew how to make tasty little dishes for Mustapha which cost him nothing. She never asked him for money. Indeed, hadn't she got herself into debt so that he would be more comfortable and have better meals at her place? And in the past, when Mustapha sometimes arrived unexpectedly – this was soon after he had married her – hadn't she hastened to make succulent dishes for him? All her friends knew this.

A comforting thought coursed through her and sent these aggressive and vindictive reflections to sleep. She told herself that Mustapha was bound to come to her this evening. The certainty of his presence stripped her mind of the too cruel thought that the time of her disfavour was approaching; this thought had been as much a burden to her as a heavy weight dragging a drowning man to the bottom. When all the bad, unfavourable thoughts besetting her had been dispersed, like piles of rubbish on waste land swept by a flood, the future seemed brighter, and she joined in the conversation of the women with childish enthusiasm, unable to hide her pleasure and her hopes. It was like something in a parcel; questioning eyes wondered what was inside, but she alone knew and enjoyed the secret, drawing an agreeable strength from it. She took an active part in the talking and brought her wit into play. All this vivacity sprang from the joyful conviction that Mustapha would arrive this evening very hungry and be hers alone.

In the far distance, high above the tree-tops, a long trail of dark-grey clouds tinged with red was hiding the sun. The time for the *tacousane*, the afternoon prayer, was drawing near. One by one, the women withdrew to their rooms, and the shadows of the trees grew longer, wider and darker.

Night fell; a dark, starry night.

Noumbe cooked some rice for the children. They clamoured in vain for some of the meat. Noumbe was stern and unyielding: 'The meat is for your father. He didn't eat at midday.' When she had fed the children, she washed herself again to get rid of the smell of cooking and touched up her toilette, rubbing oil on her hands, feet and legs to make the henna more brilliant. She intended to remain by her door, and sat down on the bench; the incense smelt strongly, filling the whole room. She was facing the entrance to the compound and could see the other women's husbands coming in.

But for her there was no one.

She began to feel tired again. Her heart was troubling her, and she had a fit of coughing. Her inside seemed to be on fire. Knowing that she would not be going to the dispensary during her 'three days', in order to economize, she went and got some wood-ash which she mixed with water and drank. It did not taste very nice, but it would make the medicine last longer, and the drink checked and soothed the burning within her for a while. She was tormenting herself with the thoughts passing through her mind. Where can he be? Everyone knew that she was out of favour with Mustapha. The third wife was herself. So he must be with the fourth. There were puckers of uncertainty and doubt in the answers she gave herself. She kept putting back the time to go to bed, like a lover who does not give up waiting when the time of the rendezvous is long past, but with an absurd and stupid hope waits still longer, self-torture and the heavy minutes chaining him to the spot. At each step Noumbe took, she stopped and mentally explored the town, prying into each house inhabited by one of the other wives. Eventually she went indoors.

SEMBENE OUSMANE   *Tribal Scars*

Questions

1 Describe *two* ways in which Mustapha is neglecting his responsibilities to Noumbe.

2 How do we know that meat is a special treat in Noumbe's home?

3 Describe all the preparations that Noumbe makes for Mustapha's visit.

4 Write out the simile in the passage that tells us that all these preparations are for nothing.

5 How do we know that Noumbe is behaving in a way that is dangerous to her health?

6 Where does the passage hint to us that Mustapha is?

7 What does the writer mean by this sentence:
'At each step Noumbe took, she stopped and mentally explored the town, prying into each house inhabited by one of the other wives.'

8 How do we know that the writer of this passage disapproves of polygamy?

9 This writer uses a lot of similes. Pick out *two others* (i.e. *not* the one you have written out in question 4). Describe what is being compared in the two similes you have chosen.

10 Find *one* word in the passage for each of the following:
- delicious and juicy
- flowed rapidly
- bright cheerfulness
- certain knowledge
- loudly begged and pleaded

11 How does the phrase 'the shadows of the trees grew longer, wider and darker' help to explain to us what Noumbe is going through?

The Joys of Motherhood

Nnu Ego and Akadu are the wives of Nnaife. Adaku is angry because Nnu Ego was rude to one of her guests to their house. She brings her complaint to two older kinsmen:

The case was stated to them, but instead of laying the whole blame on Nnu Ego, they made Adaku feel that since she had no son for the family she had no right to complain about her senior's conduct.

'Don't you know that according to the custom of our people you, Adaku, the daughter of whoever you are, are committing an unforgivable sin?' Nwakusor reminded her. 'Our life starts from immortality and ends in immortality. If Nnaife had been married to only you, you would have ended his life on this round of his visiting earth. I know you have children, but they are girls, who in a few years' time will go and help build another man's immortality. The only woman who is immortalising your husband you make unhappy with your fine clothes and lucrative business. If I were in your shoes, I should go home and consult my *chi* to find out why male offspring have been denied me. But instead, here you are quarrelling about your visitor. Why did she have to dress up so extravagantly, anyway, and during the week for that matter?'

Though Ibuza men admired a hard-working and rich woman, her life was nothing if she left no male children who were her own flesh and blood. What was the point of piling up wealth when there was nobody to leave it for?

Nwakusor had a word of caution for Nnu Ego. She must guard her reputation. Children were all very well, but they would only enjoy and glory in their parents if those parents had made sure to leave a good, clean name behind them. She should never let it be repeated that the daughter of Nwokocha Agdabi by his eternal sweetheart Ona did not know the art of courtesy to a visitor.

'Don't you realise that the house belongs to you, so why should you feel reluctant to welcome a caller, and an Ibuza woman for that matter?' Nwakusor asked.

Nnu Ego could not say that it was because the woman looked so well off, and because Adaku had been parading her own wealth ever since Nnu Ego arrived back from Ibuza. So she kept quiet, only murmuring: 'This Lagos, it makes me forget my position sometimes. It will not happen again, I promise.'

'Well you must pay a fine of a keg of palm wine and a tin of cigarettes.'

Adaku stood looking on and saw that she was completely ignored. They did not ask Nnu Ego to apologise to her, and for a time it looked as if they had even forgotten it had been she who invited them to settle the case in the first place. The message was clear: she was only a lodger, her position in Nnaife Owulum's household had not been ratified. Nor did the fact that she was making a lot of money particularly endear her to them. She got the message.

As soon as the men went, Nnu Ego crawled into her bed, which she had now covered with hand-spun mats as she had no money for bed-sheets. Her feelings were mixed, and she wanted to weep, for what she did not know. She felt sorry for Adaku, and the men's hurtful treatment of her, but would Adaku understand if she should tell her so? She also felt relief, knowing that her own fate could so easily have been like Adaku's. Yet all because she was the mother of three sons, she was supposed to be happy in her poverty, in her nail-biting agony, in her churning stomach, in her rags, in her cramped room . . . Oh, it was a confusing world.

BUCHI EMECHETA *The Joys of Motherhood*

Questions

1 Describe why Nnu Ego had become jealous of Adaku causing her to be rude to one of Adaku's guests.

2 In what way had the guest added to Nnu Ego's anger?

3 Describe in detail why the men sided with Nnu Ego. Do you think that their argument was fair? Why?

4 Describe in detail how we know that men and male children were seen to be much more important than women and female children in the society the writer describes.

5 What did the men criticise Nnu Ego for?

6 The passage is set in the big West African city of Lagos. In what way is this important to what happens in the story?

7 Describe in your own words what is meant by: 'she was only a lodger, her position in Nnaife Owulum's household had not been ratified.'

8 Why is Adaku unhappy even though she had three sons? Do you think her unhappiness is justified?

9 Write out a line in the passage that tells us that Nnu Ego is really a kind and sympathetic person.

10 What does the phrase that 'Nnu Ego crawled into her bed' tell us about how she is feeling?
11 Make sentences with the following words:
  - lucrative
  - extravagantly
  - reputation
  - relief
  - poverty.

Ramatoulaye

Modou has died. His elder brother, Tamsir, comes to ask Ramatoulaye (the person telling the story and Modou's widow) to marry him:

Tamsir speaks with great assurance; he touches, once again, on my years of marriage, then he concludes: 'When you have "come out" (that is to say, of mourning), I shall marry you. You suit me as a wife, and further, you will continue to live here, just as if Modou were not dead. Usually it is the younger brother who inherits his elder brother's wife. In this case, it is the opposite. You are my good luck. I shall marry you. I prefer you to the other one, too frivolous, too young. I advised Modou against that marriage.'

What a declaration of love, full of conceit, in a house still in mourning. What assurance and calm aplomb! I look Tamsir straight in the eye . . . I tell my beads. This time I shall speak out.

My voice has known thirty years of silence, thirty years of harassment. It bursts out, violent, sometimes sarcastic, sometimes contemptuous.

'Did you ever have any affection for your brother? Already you want to build a new home for yourself, over a body that is still warm. While we are praying for Modou, you are thinking of future wedding festivities.

'Ah, yes! Your strategy is to get in before any other suitor, to get in before Mawdo, the faithful friend, who has more qualities than you and who also, according to custom, can inherit the wife. You forget that I have a heart, a mind, that I am not an object to be passed from hand to hand. You don't know what marriage means to me: it is an act of faith and of love, the total surrender of oneself to the person one has chosen and who had chosen you.' (I emphasized the word 'chosen'.)

'What of your wives, Tamsir? Your income can meet neither their needs nor those of your numerous children. To help you out with your financial obligations, one of your wives dyes, another sells fruit, the third untiringly turns the handle of her sewing machine. You, the revered lord, you take it easy, obeyed at the crook of a finger. I shall never be the one to complete

104

your collection. My house shall never be for you the coveted oasis: no extra burden; my "turn" every day; cleanliness and luxury, abundance and calm! No, Tamsir! . . .

Much later Ramatoulaye thinks about the marriage of her daughter, Daba, to Abou:

Daba does not find household work a burden. Her husband cooks rice as well as she does; her husband who claims, when I tell him he 'spoils' his wife: 'Daba is my wife. She is not my slave, nor my servant.'

I sense the tenderness growing between this young couple, an ideal couple, just as I have always imagined. They identify with each other, discuss everything so as to find a compromise.

All the same, I fear for Daba. Life holds many surprises. When I discuss it with her, she shrugs her shoulders: 'Marriage is no chain. It is mutual agreement over a life's programme. So if one of the partners is no longer satisfied with the union, why should he remain? It may be Abou; it may be me. Why not? The wife can take the initiative to make the break.'

MARIAMA BÂ   *So Long a Letter*

Questions

1 How do we know that Tamsir fully expects Ramatoulaye to marry him?
2 Was Ramatoulaye Modou's only wife? How do we know?
3 How do we know that Ramatoulaye's marriage to Modou had not been altogether happy?
4 Describe in detail, and in your own words, why Ramatoulaye refuses Tamsir.
5 Compare the marriage situation of Tamsir and his wives to that of Daba and Abou.
6 a How do we know that Ramatoulaye does not really believe that Abou 'spoils' his wife?

  b Abou and Daba are a younger generation than Ramtoulaye and Tamsir. What do you think the writer is trying to say about marriage and the future of women in her country?

7 What is meant by:
 • obeyed at the crook of a finger
 • coveted oasis
 • marriage is no chain
 • take the initiative

8 Make sentences with the following:
 • assurance
 • harassment
 • contemptuous
 • strategy
 • compromise

What have you learnt about polygamy in the four passages looked at so far? Do you think that the writers are too negative about it? Why?

Creative writing

Re-read and think about the second passage again. Imagine that Mustapha has finally just arrived and brought two friends with him. He is expecting a great feast for all of them. Describe what happens.

or

Write a story centering around characters involved in a polygamous marriage.

The Marriage of Mihrène

Ephraim, a diamond cutter from Johannesburg flies to Egypt at the request of a wealthy merchant who wishes him to prepare a wedding gift for his daughter, Mihrène:

They were people, are people, with nothing remarkable about them but their wealth, and the enchanting Mihrène, whom Ephraim first saw in a mist of white embroidered muslin standing by a fountain, was a girl neither more pretty nor more gifted than, let's say, a dozen that evening in Alexandria, a thousand or so in Egypt, hundreds of thousands in the countries round about, all of which produce so plentifully her particular type – her beautiful type: small-boned, black-haired, black-eyed, apricot-skinned, lithe.

She had lived for twenty years in this atmosphere of well-chosen luxury; loved and bickered with her mother and her sisters; respected her papa; and was intending to marry Paulo, a young man from South America with whom she would continue to live exactly the same kind of life, only in Buenos Aires.

For her it was an ordinary evening, a family dinner at which a friend of Papa's was present. She did not know about the diamonds: they were to be a surprise. She was wearing last year's dress and a choker of false pearls: that season it was smart to wear 'costume' pearls, and to leave one's real pearls in a box on one's dressing-table.

Ephraim, son of jewellers, saw the false pearls around that neck and suffered. . . .

She was certainly bored, yawned once or twice, and did not try too hard to hide the yawns. The diamond-cutter from Johannesburg gazed at her, forgot to eat, and asked twice why she wore false pearls in a voice rough with complaint. He was gauche, she decided – and forgot him.

He did not return home, but wired for money. He had never spent any, and so had a great deal available for the single perfect pearl which he spent days looking for, and which he found at last in a back room in Cairo, where he sat bargaining over coffee cups for some days with an old Persian dealer who knew as much about gems as he did, and who would not trade in anything but the best.

With this jewel he arrived at the house of Mihrène's father, and when she was seated in a room opening on to an inner court where jasmine clothed a wall, and lily pads a pool, he asked permission to give the pearl to the young girl . . .

(Mihrène's father allows Ephraim to offer her the pearl):

She picked up the pearl from the damask, and let it lie in her palm. She, her fiancé, and her father, looked at the pearl whose value they were all well equipped to assess, and Ephraim looked sternly at the girl. Then she lifted long, feathery black lashes and looked at him – in inquiry? An appeal to be let off? His eyes were judging, disappointed; they said what his words had said: Why are you content with the second-rate?

Preposterous . . .

Impossible . . .

Finally Mihrène gave the slightest shrug of shoulders, tonight covered in pink organza, and said to Ephraim, 'Thank you, thank you very much.'
. . .

Next day he went back to Johannesbrug, and on Mihrène's dressing-table lay a small silver box in which was a single perfect pearl.

She was to marry in three weeks. . . .

When she refused to marry Paulo, quite prettily and nicely, Papa and Mamma Kantannis made ritual remarks about her folly, her ingratitude, and so forth, but in engagements like these no hearts are expected to be broken, for the marriages are like the arranged marriages of dynasties. If she did not marry Paulo, she would marry someone like him – and she was very young.

They remarked that she had not been herself since the affair of the pearl. Papa said to himself that he would see to it no more fly-by-nights arrived at his dinner-table. . . .

(Mihrène, however, falls in love with Carlos, a poor engineer, who is, moreover, very politically aware and active against the fascists led by Mussolini):

She married her Carlos in the week Paulo married a girl from a French dynasty. Mihrène went to Rome and lived in a small villa without servants, and with nothing to fall back on but the memory of a nondescript elderly man who had sat opposite her throughout two long, dull dinners and who had given her a pearl as if he were giving her a lesson. She thought that in all her life no one else had ever demanded anything of her, ever asked anything, ever taken her seriously.

DORIS LESSING   *Out of the Fountain*

Questions

1 Describe all that you have learnt about the class of people to which Mihrène belonged.

2 How do we know that Ephraim himself lived quite a different kind of life from Mihrène's?

3 Why was Mihrène wearing false pearls?

4 Describe in your own words why Ephraim was so upset by the false pearls. Remember to read through the whole passage.

5 What did he decide to do about it?

6 a What did the pearl come to mean to Mihrène?

   b What did she decide to do about it?

   c How do we know that it did not really change Paulo's life?

   d Contrast Mihrène's life with Carlos with what it would have been with Paulo.

7 Ephraim has been described in the passage as (*a*) gauche; (*b*) a fly-by-night; (*c*) a nondescript elderly man. Say what is meant by each of these in the context in which the description appears in the passage.

8 a Write out the words in the passage that tell us that Mihrène was not an exceptional, special person, not a heroine just waiting to be discovered by someone.

   b What is the writer, therefore, trying to tell all women wherever they are?

9 The writer is trying to create a romantic and exotic atmosphere in the setting of her story. Find at least *two* examples of where she does so.

10 Make sentences with the following words:
   • enchanting
   • bored
   • assess
   • preposterous
   • ingratitude

11 Find *one* word in the passage for each of the following:
   • argued
   • false (jewellery)
   • look at admiringly
   • stupidity
   • cottage

Escape

She desired, more than anything, to fly away; like a cock, which has unknotted itself from the string tying its leg to the wall. She wanted to fly away fom the dependence on the seasons, the seasons which determine the life or death of the nomads. And she wanted to fly away from the squabbles over water, squabbles caused by the lack of water, which meant that the season was bad. She wanted to go away from the duty of women. Not that she was intending to feel idle and do nothing, nor did she feel irresponsible, but a woman's duty meant loading and unloading camels and donkeys after the destination had been reached, and that life was routine: goats for girls and camels for boys got on her nerves more than she could stand. To her, this allotment of assignments denoted the status of woman, that she was lower in status than a man, and that she was weak. 'But it is only because camels are stupid beasts that boys can manage to handle them,' she always consoled herself. She loathed this discrimination between the sexes: the idea that boys lift up the prestige of the family and keep the family's name alive. Even a moron-male cost twice as much as two women in terms of blood-compensation. As many as twenty or thirty camels are allotted to each son. The women, however, have to wait until their fates give them a new status in life: the status of marriage. The she-camel is given to the son, as people say 'tied to his navel' as soon as he is born. 'Maybe God prefers men to women,' she told herself.

But Ebla had no answers to the questions how to escape, where should she escape to, whom should she go to, and when she should escape.

To escape. To be free. To be free. To be free. To escape. These were inter-related.

How to escape? Where to escape to?

Throughout the night, she had been thinking of the easiest method by which she could escape without her grandfather and her brother and the others knowing about it. Her future husband had gone away to the next dwelling, and would be back on the morrow, she had learnt the previous evening. But how? How to escape? She thought about the matter seriously, but there seemed to be no way out. The way to escape was not clear to her. Gradually the clues dripped into her mind as the spring rain drips on to the green grass with the morning dawn. Things came to light. Situations became more friendly. She knew what she should do: escape alone and join the caravan going to Belet Wene, which would leave after a while, she told herself. 'After a while,' she repeated to herself, 'After a while.' . . .

Ebla had learnt, even before she had seriously decided to fly away, that the only reasonable place she could go to would be a town. She was not sure which town would suit her best. Which place would give her all the things she wanted?

NURUDDIN FARAH *From a Crooked Rib*

Questions

1 Describe briefly and in your own words, the *three* things that Ebla wished to escape from.

2 a What are *nomads*?

  b Describe what you have learnt about the life of nomads from this passage.

3 What reason does Ebla give in order to comfort herself for the fact that it was 'goats for girls and camels for boys'?

4 a Describe the ways in which women are discriminated against among the nomads.

  b What reason for this discrimination does Ebla suggest? Do you think she is correct? Why?

5 How do we know that Ebla's marriage was probably arranged for her without her consent?

6 Why do you think 'the only reasonable place she could go to would be a town'?

7 Do you imagine that Ebla is correct in thinking that to escape from the nomads would mean that she would be entirely free from being looked down upon because she was a woman? Why?

8 What is meant by the following:
  • That life was routine
  • allotment of assignments
  • discrimination between the sexes
  • blood compensation
  • 'tied to his navel' as soon as he is born

9 Find *two* similes in the passage and describe what is being compared in each case.

10 Find *one* word in the passage for each of the following:
  • having to rely (on)
  • quarrels
  • lazy
  • comforted
  • very much hated
  • group of nomads travelling together for safety

Boys or Girls?

Sissie is from Ghana, and is in Germany on a travelling scholarship. She befriends a young German housewife called Marija:

She (Marija) had already informed Sissie that Adolf was going to be her only child. There had been complications with his birth and the Herr Doktor had advised her not to attempt to have another child. It might be unsafe for her. And now smiling even more broadly, she said that since Adolf was going to be the only child, she was very happy he was a boy.

Any good woman
In her senses
With her choices
Would say the
Same

In Asia
Europe
Anywhere:

For
Here under the sun,
Being a woman
Has not
Is not
Cannot
Never will be a
Child's game

From knowledge gained since –

So why wish a curse on your child
Desiring her to be female
?
Beside, my sister,
The ranks of the wretched are
Full,
Are full.

AMA ATA AIDOO *Our Sister Killjoy*

Questions

1 Why was Adolf going to be Marija's only child?
2 a Why is Marija so happy that Adolf is a boy?
  b For what reason does Sissie agree that any mother should desire a boy?
  c Do you think, however, that Sissie is being a bit ironic (using irony, not really believing what she is appearing to be saying) when she insists that mothers should want sons? Why?
3 How do we know that Marija's attitude is one that Sissie has come across in Africa?
4 Write out the line that tells us that certain attitudes to women have existed for a long, long time.
5 What does the writer mean by saying that being a woman
'Never will be a
Child's game'?

111

6 a What do you think is the effect of Sissie expressing her thoughts in poetry?

  b What is the effect of the repetition in the last two lines of the poem:
'Full,
Are full.'?

7 Why do you think Sissie refers to 'my sister' in the poem?

8 Write out the line that tells us that the writer is linking the suffering of women to the suffering of all oppressed people. Do you think she is correct to do this? Why?

9 Make sentences with the following words:
- complications
- curse
- ranks
- wretched

Further discussion

1 What are some similarities and differences between Mihrène and Ebla?

2 Look again at the last three passages. Pick out some of the most important points they are making about the situation of women in general and their possibilities for the future. (You do not need to use all three passages in your answer).

Creative writing

Carry on the story *either* of Ebla *or* Mihrène.

or

Write your own story of a woman who is trapped and unhappy with her life, and who tries to change it in some way.

Book list

MONGO BETI *Perpetua and the Habit of Unhappiness*, Heinemann, 1978, pp. 27 – 9, & 190.

SEMBENE OUSMANE 'Her Three Days', in *Tribal Scars*, Heinemann, 1974, pp. 43 – 4.

BUCHI EMECHETA *The Joys of Motherhood,* Heinemann, 1979, pp. 166–7.

MARIAMA BÂ *So Long a Letter*, Heinemann, 1981, pp. 57 – 8 & 73 – 4.

DORIS LESSING 'Out of the Fountain', in *The Story of a Non-Marrying Man*, Penguin, 1975, pp. 14 – 20.

NURUDDIN FARAH *From a Crooked Rib*, Heinemann, 1970, pp. 13 – 14.

AMA ATA AIDOO *Our Sister Killjoy*, Longman, 1977, pp. 50 – 1.

South Africans P. Róhr-Rouendaal

Race

In this final chapter we come to what is perhaps one of the most painful topics to consider – that of racial prejudice, and we see what some of the writers have to say about it. We look first at four versions of racism that occur in very different racial situations.

Most of the writers are concerned with showing the terrible effects of racism on people's lives. Few writers try and look deeply into causes *of racism. These causes are, of course, very complicated. One writer who does seek to explain the causes is Ngugi wa Thiong'o. We will look at what he has to say in the final passage of the chapter.*

South African writers and situations are presented more than others in this chapter. This is to be expected given the system of Apartheid.

Read through the passages and answer the questions carefully. Think also about situations of racial prejudice that you have experienced or heard about, and try to understand better their effects and causes.

Versions of Racism – 1:
I entertain fine company

The following is a description of some Afrikaners by an Englishman. The extract is taken from a book published a long time ago:

It was some time before I caught sight of the approaching horsemen. At last they showed themselves, as they came riding slowly over the brow of a small hillock about a hundred yards away from the waggon. I could make out that they were three Boers – dirty, ugly specimens of a dirty race. Their unkempt hair hung down on to their shoulders . . . They were dressed in corduroys, the trousers being very short and baggy, exposing their dirty, unstockinged ankles, while their jackets only reached down to about their waists. Their faces were covered by rough bushy beards, and looked as if they had not been washed for a year – very likely true, as your Boer hates water. Each man carried a rifle and a bandolier of cartridges hung over his shoulder. They rode slowly up to my waggon and dismounted, leaving their horses to graze near. Then, after the manner of their countrymen, each one came to me in turn and held out his dirty hand, straight from the elbow, then dropped it into mine as if it were a dead fish. This is their idea of shaking hands. When this ordeal was over, the three of them sat down by me, and, without saying a word, took out their tobacco bags, filled and lighted their pipes, and gazed stupidly before them. Whilst they were thus engaged, I had time to examine them a little more closely . . .

The kettle was soon boiling, and the coffee made. I produced three other tin pannikins, and poured it out. The one by the fire being by far the biggest, I handed it to the giant, and said with a smile:

'The biggest cup must go to the biggest man.'

'No, no,' he replied, 'I am not thirsty; give me the small one, and take this one yourself, for why would I take your cup?'

This was certainly the greatest piece of politeness and magnaminity I had ever entertained from any Boer, for by long experience I knew they would take all they could get.

GEORGE HANSBY RUSSEL   *Under the Sjambok*

Questions

1 The title of the passage is the writer's title for his chapter. In what way can the writer be said to be being *ironic* in his title?

2 Find all the examples you can which show us that the writer is racially prejudiced against 'the Boers'.

3 Describe in your own words the appearance and dress of the Boers.

4 Describe two ways in which the writer shows this dislike of the men's way of shaking hands.

5 a What politeness does the very big man show the writer?

  b How do you think the writer would explain this politeness?

6 What is
- a hillock
- a speciman
- cartridges

7 Find one word in the passage for
- untidy
- unpleasant experience
- a cup
- generosity

8 Re-write in indirect speech the conversation between the writer and 'the giant'.

Versions of Racism – 2: A Roadgang's Cry

Pneumatic drills
roar like guns in a battlefield
as they tear the street.

Puffing machines swallow the red soil
and spit it out like a tuberculotic's sputum.

Business-bent brokers hurry past;
Women shoppers shamble tiredly, shooing their children;
Stragglers stop to stare
as the ruddy-faced foreman watches men
lifting a sewerage pipe into a trench.

It starts
as a murmur
from one mouth to another
in a rhythm of ribaldry
that rises to a crescendo
**'Abelungu ngo'dam
Basibiza ngo Jim –**
Whites are damned
they call us Jim.'

OSWALD MBUYISENI MTSHALI   *A Roadgang's Cry*

Questions

1 Describe in detail what the men of the roadgang are doing.

2 Describe in your own words the people who walk past them.

3 How do you know that the workers are most likely singing in their own language?

4 How do we know that the foreman is a white man?

5 Explain what is meant by 'they call us Jim'.

6 Why are the last lines of the poem such a dramatic climax, one that we have not really been led to expect from the earlier verses?

7 Pneumatic drills and 'puffing machines' are each compared to something in a simile.

   a Describe what they are being compared to in each case.

   b Which comparison do you prefer? Why?

8 Find a word in the poem that means
- spittle
- walk in an awkward, shuffling way
- walkers who are not in a great hurry to get anywhere
- irreverent (daring, disrespectful) joking
- great climax of noise

9 Now choose *three* of the words that you have found in answer to question 8 and make sentences with them.

Versions of Racism – 3: Black Girl

Sissie has come to Germany from Africa on a travelling scholarship:

Suddenly, she realised a woman was telling a young girl who must have been her daughter:

   'Ja, das Schwartze Mädchen.'

From the little German that she had been advised to study for the trip, she knew that 'das Schwartze Mädchen meant 'black girl'.

   She was somewhat puzzled.

   Black girl? Black girl?

So she looked around her, really well this time.

And it hit her. That all that crowd of people going and coming in all sorts of directions had the colour of the pickled pig parts that used to come from foreign places to the markets at home.

Trotters, pig-tails, pig-ears.

She looked and looked at so many of such skins together.

And she wanted to vomit.

Then she was ashamed of her reaction.

Something pulled inside of her.

For the rest of her life, she was to regret this moment when she was made to notice differences in human colouring.

Later, Sissie has a meal with a German woman, Marija, and she has this to say about the food:

(She) Brought out the cold cuts. Sliced cold ham. Sliced cold lamb. Pieces of cold chicken meat. Sliced cold sausages. Sliced cheese. Picked olives. Pickled gherkins. Sauerkraut. Strange looking foods that tasted even stranger. Each of them stone cold. Yet all of them pulled out from the fridge or some corner of the kitchen with a loving familiarity.

Sissie would always puzzle over it. Cold food. Even after she had taught her tongue to accept them, she could never really understand why people ate cold food. To eat ordinary cooked food that has gone cold without bothering to heat it is unpleasant enough. But to actually chill food in order to eat it was totally beyond her understanding. In the end, she decide it had something to do with white skins, cornsilk hair and very cold weather.

AMA ATA AIDOO   Our Sister Killjoy

Questions

1 a Write out a sentence from the passage that tells us that this was the first time that Sissie had become colour conscious.

  b Why is Sissie puzzled at the words 'black girl'?

2 a How does Sissie describe white skins as looking?

  b What effect does the appearance of Whites have on her?

  c Do you think she is correct to feel ashamed of her reaction? Why?

3 Write out the sentence that tells us that Marija enjoyed cold food.

4 a What explanation does Sissie give for this enjoyment?

  b What do you think of Sissie's explanation? Why?

5 Describe in your own words the meaning of:
   - 'Something pulled inside of her'
   - 'Even after she had taught her tongue to accept them . . .'

6 Do you think that Sissie can herself be called racially prejudiced against Europeans? Why?

Versions of Racism – 4:
I'm not ashamed of being a Masarwa

Margaret Cadmore was born into an outcast tribe in Botswana sometimes called insultingly Masarwa or Bushmen by the Batswana. She was adopted by a White woman after her own mother had died in childbirth.

It was only when she started going to the mission school that she slowly became aware that something was wrong with her relationship to the world. She was the kind of child who was slyly pinched under the seat, and next to whom no one wanted to sit.

It was odd, because she had a vantage point from which she could observe the behaviour of a persecutor. What did it really mean when another child walked up to her and, looking so angry, said: 'You are just a Bushman'? In their minds it meant so much. Half of it was that they were angry that she had the protection of a white woman who was also their principal. What was the other half? What was a Bushman supposed to do? She had no weapons of words or personality, only a permanent silence and a face which revealed no emotion, except that now and then an abrupt tear would splash down out of one eye. If a glob of spit dropped onto her arm during the playtime hour, she quietly wiped it away. If they caught her in some remote part of the school buildings during the playtime hour, they would set up the wild, jiggling dance: 'Since when did a bushy go to school? We take him to the bush where he eat mealie pap, pap, pap. . . .'

Margaret qualifies as a teacher, and is appointed to her first post in a remote, inland village called Dilepe. There she meets another teacher called Dikeledi:

Dikeledi looked down. A slight frown flitted across her face. It was the first time the other had spoken and she could not quite place her in the scheme of things. The near perfect English accent and manners did not fit her looks. In fact, not one thing about her fitted another and she looked half like a Chinese and half like an African and half like God knows what.

'What's your name?' she asked at last.

'Margaret Cadmore,' the other said.

'Is your father a white man?' asked Dikeledi.

Since the atmosphere between them was so relaxed, the other young girl spoke without hesitation:

'No', she said. 'Margaret Cadmore was the name of my teacher. She was a white woman from England. I am a Masarwa.'

Dikeledi drew in her breath with a sharp, hissing sound. Dilepe village was the stronghold of some of the most powerful and wealthy chiefs in the country, all of whom owned innumerable Masarwa as slaves.

'Don't mention this to anyone else,' she said, shock making her utter strange words. 'If you keep silent about the matter, people will simply assume you are a Coloured . . .'

'But I am not ashamed of being a Masarwa,' the young girl said seriously. 'Let me show you something.'

She opened her handbag and took out a small, framed picture.

'My teacher made this sketch of my mother the day she died,' she said, and handed it to Dikeledi. Dikeledi took the picture, glanced at it with that strange, wide stare, then looked away into the distance, an almost smoky haze clouding her lovely eyes.

'Did a white woman write that?' she asked. 'And about a Masarwa? 'She looks like a Goddess?'

Her face suddenly broke into a pretty, shy smile.

'I am not like you, Margaret,' she said. 'I am afraid to protest about anything because life easily overwhelms me, but you are right to tell anyone that you are a Masarwa.'

BESSIE HEAD   *Maru*

Questions

1 Describe in your own words *all* the ways in which the other children were nasty to Margaret.

2 What are the *two* reasons the writer suggests for this nastiness?

3 How did Margaret respond to the ill-treatment of her by the other children?

4 How do we know that it was unusual for a child like Margaret to be in school in the first place?

5 Why was Dikeledi puzzled when she first met Margaret?

6 How do we know that Margaret did not always immediately tell people that she was a Masarwa?

7 How do you think the chiefs of Dilepe village would feel about a Masarwa teaching their children? Why would they feel this? (Look carefully in the passage for your answer.)

8 a What advice does Dikeledi give Margaret, and what does Dikeledi later say about herself that helps to explain why she gives it?

   b Why does Margaret disagree with this advice? Do you think she is correct? Why?

9 Why is Dikeledi surprised at the words Margaret Cadmore (senior) had written on the sketch of Margaret's mother?

10 Make sentences with the following words:
    - slyly
    - persecutor
    - abrupt
    - innumerable
    - overwhelms

11 What are the meanings of the following phrases:
- 'something was wrong with her relationship to the world'
- 'she had a vantage point from which she could observe the behaviour of a persecutor'
- 'she had no weapons of words or personality'
- 'she could not quite place her in the scheme of things'

Further discussion

1 a We have seen four different versions or situations of racism. Can you think of other examples such as North Americans' attitudes towards American Indians?

b What conclusions, if any, do you think can be drawn from the fact that there are so many different racist situations?

2 Which passage struck you most forcefully? Why?

Creative writing

Describe what happens in Margaret's classroom after her pupils find out about her racial origins.
or
Write your own story or poem centering around a racist incident or racism in general.

Black and White Together – 1: The Disillusionment

Rosa Burger's father died in jail in South Africa, where he was being detained as a political prisoner. She is in London on a visit. At a party she bumps into a young Black man who, as a boy, had been taken into the Burger household. After the party they have this telephone conversation:

The voice from home said: Rosa.
– Yes. –
– Yeh, Rosa. –
– It's you, Baasie? –
– No. – A long, swaying pause.
– But it is. –
– I'm not 'Baasie', I'm Zwelinzima Vulindlela. –
– I'm sorry – it just came out this evening . . . it was ridiculous. –
– You know what my name means, Rosa? –
– Vulindlela? Your father's name . . . oh, I don't know whether my surname means anything either – 'citizen', solid citizen – Starting to

humour the other one; at such an hour – too much to drink, perhaps.
– Zwel-in-zima. That's my name. 'Suffering land'. The name my father gave me. . . .

– Listen. I didn't like the things you said at that place tonight. –
– *I* said? –
– I didn't like the way you went around and how you spoke. –
  The receiver took on shape and feel in her hand; blood flowing to her brain. She heard his breathing and her own, her breath breathing garlic over herself from the half-digested sausage.
– I don't know what to say. I don't understand why you should say this to me. –
– Look, I didn't like it at all. –
– I said? About what? –
– Lionel Burger, Lionel Burger, Burger –
– I didn't make any speeches. –
– Everyone in the world must be told what a great hero he was and how much he suffered for the blacks. Everyone must cry over him and show his life on television and write in the papers. Listen, there are dozens of our fathers sick and dying like dogs, kicked out of the locations when they can't work any more. Getting old and dying in prison. Killed in prison. It's nothing. I know plenty blacks like Burger. It's nothing, it's us, we must be used to it, it's not going to show on English television. –
  He would have been the first to say – what you're saying. He didn't think there was anything special about a white being a political prisoner. –
– Kissing and coming round you, her father died in prison, how terrible. I know a lot of fathers – black –
– He didn't think what happened to him more important. –
– Kissing and coming round you –
– You knew him! You know that! It's crazy for me to tell *you*.
– Oh yes I knew him. You'll tell them to ask me for the television show. Tell them how your parents took the little black kid into their home, not the backyard like other whites, right into the house. Eating at the table and sleeping in the bedroom, the same bed, their little black boss. And then the little bastard was pushed off back to his mud huts and tin shanties. His father was too busy to look after him. Always on the run from the police.
. . .
  She hunched the thing to her head, clasping with the other hand the wrist of the hand that held it. – Where did they take you when you left us? Why won't you tell me? It was Transkei? Oh God. King William's Town? And I suppose you know – perhaps you didn't – Tony drowned. At home. –
– But he taught us to swim. –
– Diving. Head hit the bottom of the pool. –
– No, I didn't hear. Your little boss-kid that was one of the family couldn't make much use of the lessons, there was no private swimming-pool the places I stayed. –

123

– Once we'd left that kindergarten there wasn't any school you could have gone to in our area. What could your father or mine do about that. My mother didn't want your father to take you at all. –

– What was so special about me? One black kid? Whatever you whites touch, it's a take-over. He was my father. Even when we get free they'll want us to remember to thank Lionel Burger. –. . .

She was shouting. – How could you follow me around that room like a man from BOSS*, listening to stupid small-talk? Why are we talking in the middle of the night? Why do you telephone? What for? –

- I'm not your Baasie, just don't go on thinking about that little kid who lived with you, don't think of that black 'brother', that's all. –

NADINE GORDIMER   *Burger's Daughter*

Questions

1 Why is the man so angry that the Burgers never knew him by his African name? (Rosa later cannot pronounce the word 'Zwelinzima'.)

2 Why is he so bitter towards the Burger family generally, even though he grew up as an equal in their home for part of his childhood? (Think carefully about the passage as a whole for your answer. Think about what the child was used to in the Burger household and what he went to afterwards).

3 a What kinds of things are being done to publicise Lionel Burger's life and death?

  b Why is Zwelinzima so resentful (bitter, angry) of the fuss made of Lionel Burger?

4 Why did Zwelinzima have to leave the Burgers?

5 There are *two* kinds of tragedy pointed to in the passage –

  a that caused by the specific political set-up of South Africa and

  b a more general kind that can occur anywhere. Give one example of both a and b.

6 What do you think Zwelinzima is trying to achieve in speaking to Rosa in this way?

7 What is *your* opinion concerning the argument they are having?

8 What is the effect created by all the dashes ' – ' in the passage?

9 What is the meaning of the following:
  • starting to humour the other one
  • whatever you whites touch, it's a take-over
  • stupid small-talk

10 Re-write in indirect speech from 'Listen. I didn't like the things you said at that place tonight' until 'It's crazy for me to tell *you*.'

*BOSS = Bureau of State Security.

124

Black and White Together – 2: United

Domingos Xavier is a tractor driver on a construction site during the Portuguese occupation of Angola. He has this conversation with his friend, Sousinha about a White engineer, Silvester, who is also working on the site:

The trust in the engineer Silvester, the machine technician, whom all the people in the encampment addressed as Mr Engineer, was of long standing. It dated from the time when Domingos, still a child merely learning to grease and clean the tractors of the Sugar Company, had heard a conversation which encouraged him to go up to the technician and always to seek a job on the site where he would be working. . . .

Domingos moved the rock on which he sat closer to the other and, changing his voice to a light hum to merge into the other noises of the *sanzala**, he whispered:

'I know that you are close to Silvester. That engineer puts a lot of trust in you, I can tell you! Where he goes, I go too. Where he goes, he always manages a slot for me. He says that I am a good tractor driver. There was the time when they put me on the night shift. For a month the shift wasn't changed; only the whites had day shifts, but for me and Carlitos never! I complained to the foreman, he wanted to dock me half a day's pay. With that, I went to speak to the engineer . . . .'

Sousinha, leaning towards his friend and gripped by the clear and direct words of the tractor driver, was nodding his head in approval. Domingos Xavier, taking pride in his connection, explained:

'You understand, brother! He isn't one of those whites who looks after you so that you will like him, or to feel good out of sentimentality. No! I know that sort well, *mano* Sousa. I know that sort very well . . . If one day you miss out on raising your hat, they are straightaway saying that you are ungrateful, all the blacks are the same, and they end up sending you to the Post. This man isn't like that, friend Sousa! . . .

In Domingos Xavier's quiet voice the engineer came to life with his slight, nervous look, his glasses with their lenses, his habitual shorts, his quick, smiling talk.

'He didn't dock anyone's pay without hearing the foreman and the aggrieved man. It was like a court. Heavens, how many times the foreman had to back down! . . .'

The tractor driver supported his tale with details, quoted instances, imitated the engineer in his poor *Kimbundu* with its Portuguese accent. But Sousinha impatiently lit his pipe, drew two puffs, and pressed:

'Go on with the story, *mano*, go on! I know all that already, I know it well. . . .'

---

*Sanzala – an African settlement possibly smaller than a village.

'It was just like I am talking to you, Sousa. One day he put his hand on my shoulder and said: "Domingos, you are a good tractor driver. But more important, you are a good man, a good Angolan." Word of honour, *mano* Sousa, word of honour! My heart went into my mouth when he said this. I'd never heard anything like that said by a white man. Then, when I was going away, he said to me very softly: "You understand, Domingos, I too am an Angolan. Study! If you can, study. You will be a good engineer." And he went off quickly, with that knack of his. I can't forget, *mano* Sousa, I can't!'

JOSÉ LUANDINO VIEIRA   *The Real Life of Domingos Xavier*

Questions

1 Why is Domingos so sure that he can trust Silvester?

2 Give an example of racial discrimination on a site that Domingos describes to his friend.

3 Explain in detail and in your own words, the way in which Domingos distinguishes (points to differences) between Silvester and other Whites.

4 a Describe Silvester's appearance in your own words.

   b What do you learn about the type of person he is from this description?

5 How does Silvester settle disputes?

6 a How do we know that Silvester is Portuguese?

   b What does he then mean by saying that he, too, is Angolan?

   c Why do you think that he whispers this somewhat secretively to Domingos?

   d Write out a line elsewhere in the passage that shows that people have to talk about certain matters secretively.

7 a What is Silvester's advice to Domingos?

   b Do you think it is good advice? Why?

8 What is the meaning of:
- of long standing
- he always manages a slot for me.
- dock me . . . pay
- (he) had to back down
- my heart went into my mouth

9 Now make sentences with each of these phrases so as to make their meaning clear.

10 Re-write from 'It was just like I am talking to you . . .' to the end of the passage in indirect speech. (You should not have any inverted commas in your answer).

126

Further discussion

The last two passages both describe White people who do not behave typically (in the most usual way) of their colour and social class. The first is concerned with the situation of Apartheid in South Africa, the second with Portuguese colonialism in Angola. Compare and contrast the situations they describe and the conclusions they are hinting at.

Creative writing

Write a discription of the people, atmosphere, incidents etc. at the party attended by Rosa Burger.
or
Write your own story of *Black and White Together*.

The Competition

A big competition has been arranged among the local Kenyan wealthy class to judge who is the biggest thief among them – i.e. who has stolen the most from the poor majority of Kenyans. The rules for the competition are being laid down:

'The second rule is this: no one without a big belly and fat cheeks should bother to come up here to waste our time. Who could possibly argue the size of a man's belly and cheeks is not the true measure of his wealth?'

Those thieves who boasted large paunches gave him a big ovation. The slim ones shouted him down. The crowd in the cave split into two, and heated arguments developed between the clan of the fatties and the clan of the skinnies.

One man who was particularly thin jumped to his feet to disassociate himself completely from the second rule. He was so angry that his Adam's apple danced up and down at tremendous speed as he talked. He argued that although it was true that many thieves and robbers had great paunches and fat cheeks that were nourished by property, there were others whose stomachs were sunken and whose cheeks were hollow because they were always thinking about the problems raised by the extent of their wealth. 'Yes', the problems associated with its very size!' the man said, and added: 'But that doesn't mean that they aren't experts in theft and robbery. A man shouldn't be discriminated against because he is thin. He can't graft an extra stomach on to himself or borrow the swollen belly of his pregnant wife so as to be allowed to take part in the competition. To be slim is not the same as being sliced thin by misfortune . . . and you don't judge a hero by the size of his calves.' The man finished and sat down. The clan of skinnies clapped vigorously, and the clan of fatties shouted him down. . . .

Then a man stood up who was neither fat nor slim. He settled the dispute by saying: 'Let us not concern ourselves with thinness or fatness, whiteness or blackness, tallness or shortness. There is no bird of prey that is to small when it comes to hunting. Anyone who feels he has what it takes should be allowed to come forward and compete with other eaters. An eater and an eater should meet in the battlefield to settle all doubt about who calls the tune in eating other people's property. Just look at our foreign guests. Some are fat; other are slim. Some have red hair; others have hair which is not so red. One comes from Japan in Asia; others come from Europe; and their leader comes from the USA. What makes them of one age-group, one house, one clan, one umbilical cord, one kind is not slimness or fatness or language. No, what binds them together, uniting them as members of one clan, is theft, which has permitted them to spread their tentacles over the whole of the Earth, like the creeping plant that crawls into all corners of the field. Therefore we, their local watchdogs, are also of one umbilical cord, one age-group, one house, one clan, one kind. We who have gathered here today, whether Luo, or Kallenjin, or Mkamba, or Mswahili, or Mmaasai, or Mkikuyu, or Mbaluhya, are brothers in theft and robbery, related to one another through our links with these foreign experts. Master of ceremonies! We all belong to one organization. Let us always remain united. It is only among the people from whom we steal that we should create divisions of tribe and religion, so that they will never develop their own strong, united organizations to oppose us. . . . You people, a fire that blazes fiercely may destroy the meat whose fate made it jump into the flames!'

NGUGI WA THIONG'O   *Devil on the Cross*

Questions

1 a In your own words, give the suggested second rule of the competition.
   b Describe briefly the argument of the thin man against this rule.
2 Explain how the writer is poking fun at those who see skin colour as the most important division between people by describing 'the clan of the fatties and the clan of the skinnies'?
3 What are some of the differences that exist between people pointed to by the man who settled the argument, besides that of size?
4 What does he suggest is the most important thing that unites the foreigners despite some of these differences?
5 What does he suggest unites the wealthy Kenyan people who have entered the competition?
6 Why does he suggest that they should create divisions among the poor?
7 The writer is using *satire* – i.e. he is poking fun at the wealthy class of Kenyans by setting up what seems to be an absurd (unreal, bizarre, strange) situation – that of a competition of thieves. He is doing this, however, in order *seriously* to criticise these people.

a What is his main point of criticism against them?

b Do you think his use of satire is effective (striking, successful)? Why?

8 Describe in your own words the meanings of the following:

- There is no bird of prey that is too small when it comes to hunting.
- to settle all doubt about who calls the tune
- (It is) theft, which has permitted them to spread their tentacles over the whole of the Earth, like the creeping plant that crawls into all corners of the field.
- a fire that blazes fiercely may destroy the meat whose fat made it jump into the flames!'

9 a Find a word in the passage that means each of the following:

- a fat stomach
- loud applause, clapping
- made big and fat
- insert or fix onto a piece of the body
- fight against, disagree with

b Now choose *three* of the words you have chosen and make sentences with them.

Further discussion

1 The writer seems to be saying that there are many differences (of race, tribe, appearance) between people but that we must understand the most important one – that which divides the rich from the poor. Do you agree? Why?

2 The writer is suggesting that divisions along tribal or religious lines are not so much the result of human nature (i.e. part of the way humans always behave), but that they have *social* causes and results. He feels that they help to divert (remove) attention from that real division between rich and poor. Do you agree? (Think also of earlier passages in this chapter).

Book list

GEORGE HANSBY RUSSEL *Under the Sjambok*, John Murrey, 1899, pp. 44–5 & 47–8.

OSWALD MBUYISENI MTSHALI 'A Roadgang's Cry', in *Sounds of a cowhide drum*, Oxford University Press, 1972, p. 13.

AMA ATA AIDOO *Our Sister Killjoy*, Longman, 1966, pp. 12–13 & 68.

BESSIE HEAD *Maru*, Heinemann, 1972, pp. 17–8 & 23–5.

JOSÉ LUANDINO VIEIRA *The Real Life of Domingos Xavier*, Heinemann, 1978, pp. 11 & 13–14.

NADINE GORDIMER *Burger's Daughter*, Jonathan Cape, 1979, pp. 318, 319–20, 320–1.

NGUGI WA THIONG'O *Devil on the Cross*, Heinemann, 1982, pp. 96–7.

ACKNOWLEDGEMENTS

We are grateful to the following for permission to reproduce copyright material:

Allison & Busby Ltd for an extract from pp. 166–7 *The Joys of Motherhood* by Buchi Emecheta; the author, Ama Ata Aidoo for extracts from pp. 16, 17, 18 – 19 *No Sweetness Here*, pub. Longman 1970; authors agents for extracts from pp. 30, 92–3 *This Earth My Brother* by Kofi Awooner, pub. Heinemann; authors agents for extracts from *Mission to Kala*, pub. Heinemann, © Mongo Beti 1964 and an extract from *Perpetua and the Habit of Unhappiness*, © Mongo Beti 1978; Jonathan Cape Limited for extracts from *Burger's Daughter* by Nadine Gordimer; Rex Collings Ltd for extracts from pp. 136, 174, 176 *Season of Anomy* by Wole Soyinka; A.D. Donker for extracts from *A Life to Live* by Yvonne Burgess; East African Publishing House for extracts from *Song of Lawino* by Okot p'Bitek; Faber and Faber Ltd for extracts from *Down Second Avenue* by Ezekiel Mphahlele; Fontana Books for extracts from *The African Child* by Camara Laye, first published by Collins; authors agents for extracts from pp. 17 – 18, 22 – 25 *Maru* by Bessie Head, pub. Heinemann Educational 1972, © Bessie Head 1971; Heinemann Educational Books for extracts from *Petals of Blood, Devil on the Cross* and *Secret Lives* by Ngugi wa Thiong'o, an extract from *The River Between* by James Ngugi, an extract from *From a Crooked Rib* by Nuruddin Farah, an extract from *Luanda* by José Luandino Vieira, extracts from *Kill Me Quick* by Meja Mwangi, extracts from *The Beautyful Ones Are Not yet Born* by Ayi Kwei Armah, extracts from *The Real Life of Domingos Xavier* by José Luandino Vieira (translated by Michael Wolfers), and for extracts from *The Promised Land, Chaiba The Algerian, Her Three Days* and *Tribal Scars* by Sembene Ousmane (These stories first appeared in *Voltaique*, pub. Présence Africaine, Paris, 1962.); Les Nouvelles Editions Africaines for an extract from *So Long a Letter* By Mariama Ba; Les Presses de la Cité for extracts from *God's Bits of Wood* by Sembene Ousmane; authors agents for an extract from *Out of the Fountain*, pub. Penguin, © Doris Lessing 1972; Longman Group Ltd for extracts from *Violence* by Festus Iyayi in 'Drumbeats' series, and extracts from *Our Sister Killjoy,* by Ama Ata Aidoo; Mbari Club for poem 'Rulers' by Mbella Sonne Dipoko, first published in *Black Orpheus* 20; the author Es'kia Mphahlele for extracts from *The Wanderers*; John Murray (Publishers) Ltd for extracts from *Under the Sjambok* by George Hansby Russel; the author, Gabriel Okara for his poem 'Piano and Drums'; Oxford University Press for 'A Roadgang's Cry' (p. 13) from *Sounds of a Cowhide Drum* by Mbuyiseni Oswald Mtshali, © Mbuyiseni Oswald Mtshali 1971, and 'The Lion and the Jewel' (pp. 8–10) from *Collected Plays 2* by Wole Soyinka, ©Wole Soyinka 1974; Ravan Press (Pty) Ltd for extracts from *Chirundu* by Es'kia Mphahlele and *We shall sing for the fatherland* by Zakes Mda; the author David Rubadiri for his poem 'Stanley Meets Mutesa'.

We have unfortunately been unable to trace the copyright owners of the extract from 'The Boy with the Tennis Racket' from *The Critic*, and would appreciate any information which would enable us to do so.